Stopwatch

Student's Book & Workbook

6

Viviane Kirmeliene

Richmond

58 St Aldates
Oxford
OX1 1ST
United Kingdom

Stopwatch Student's Book Level 6

First Edition: August 2016
ISBN: 978-607-06-1239-8

© Text: Viviane Kirmeliene
© Richmond Publishing, S.A. de C.V. 2016
Av. Río Mixcoac No. 274, Col. Acacias,
Del. Benito Juárez, C.P. 03240, Ciudad de Mexico

Publisher: Justine Piekarowicz
Editorial Team: Miroslava Guerra
Design Team: Jaime Ángeles, Karla Avila
Erick López
Pre-Press Coordinator: Daniel Santillán
Pre-Press Team: Susana Alcántara, Virginia Arroyo
Cover Design: Karla Avila
Cover Photograph: © **Shutterstock.com**

Illustrations: Tomás Benítez pp. 33, 72; Idoia Iribertegui pp. 78, 79; Berenice Muñiz pp. 24; Ismael Vásquez pp. 10, 17, 21, 28, 43, 61, 72, 91, 101

Photographs: © **Shutterstock.com:** Zeynep Demir p. 8, 32 (iPhone 6), catwalker p. 8 (Bob Marley), Igor Bulgarin p. 8 (Drama Theatre), Kobby Dagan p. 21 (Zuni tribe), Georgios Kollidas p. 30 (Nicola Tesla), Steve Mann p. 30 (Virgin Galactic), Featureflash Photo Agency p. (Richard Branson), Canadapanda p. 31 (iMac), Denys Prykhodov p. 31 (Internet search), charnsitr p. 31 (Galaxy S6 Edge), MikeDotta p. 34 (logog of the The MIT), Mark Schwettmann p. 39 (Christ the Redeemer), marekuliasz p. 43 (DJI F550 Flame Wheel), photo.ua p. 44 (Piazza San Marco), Christian Bertrand p. 45 (Actors play Commedia), Steven Collins p. 48 (Restaurant-Thailand), Patryk Kosmider p. 48 (Ships destroyed by tsunami), Steven Collins p. (car dragged by tsunami), marekuliasz p. 52 (DJI F550 Flame Wheel), JFs Pic Factory p. 59 (Electric Bicycles), Anton_Ivanov p. 80 (E.T.), Roman Vukolov p. 85 (The old Nokia), neftali p. 85 (Berlin Wall), coxy58 p. 88 (Re-enactment of World War 2), Kiev.Victor p. 90 (Monument of Discoveries) Fulcanelli p. 90 (Vasco da Gama Monument), StockPhotosArt p. 90 (Pedro Alvares Cabral statue), Thinglass p. 91 (Kindle Touch Reader), Drop of Light p. 92 (United Nations Building), Davide Calabresi p. 94 (Ebola emergency simulation), arindambanerjee p. 94 (A Valley Of Broken Houses), xdrew p. 94 (Physicist at the control desk of the ATLAS experiment), HUANG Zheng p. 97 (The Gayant Festival Takes Place), Pierre Jean Durieu p. 104 (Trinity College), littleny p. 104 (Galway, Ireland), EQRoy p. 106 (Massachusetts Institute of Technology), Jeff Whyte p. 106 (Calgary transit bus at UofC), Lena Ivashkevich p. 108 (The Carnival Parade), samzsolti p. 143 (Komarom, Hungary) Regien Paassen p. 146 (graffiti portrait of Che Guevara), TK Kurikawa p. 149 (Anti Nuclear Occupy Tent), Steve Mann p. 161 (The Futuristic Virgin Galactic Reuseable), antb p. 165 (Apple iMac)

© **AFP Forum:** ARCHIVES DU 7EME ART / PHOTO12 Colin p. 80 (The Twilight Saga: Breaking Dawn - Part 2) KOBAL / THE PICTURE DESK p. 80 (White Zombie (1932)), McPherson/AFP p. 85 (GB-Clonage-Dolly) © **Wikipedia.org.com** Kano Computing p. 35 (Kelvin Doe), Louis Bachrach p. 40 (Thomas Alva Edison), Niccolò Caranti p. 42 (Christopher Paolini), Savyasachi p. 46 (Laura Dekker), Lighthouse Roter Sand p. 46 (Segeljacht "Guppy" in Den Osse), Unknown p. 74 (Agatha Christie en 1925), ImageShack p. 80 (The Grudge poster), Official photographer p. 83 (Professor Alexander Fleming), Creative Commons Attribution p. 83 (EDSAC I, W. Renwick, M.V. Wilkes), Copyright held by the publisher or the artist p. 86 (Book Cover The Man in the High Castle), (NASA) under Photo ID: Ap11-s69-31740 p. 96 (Apollo 11 crew portrait)
© **Mercy & Canuche** p. 63 (Augustenborg Botanical Garden is a Red)

Images used under license from © **Shutterstock.com** and © **AFP Forum**
All rights reserved. No part of this work may be reproduced, stored in a retrieval system or transmitted in any form or by any means without prior written permission from the Publisher.

Richmond publications may contain links to third party websites or apps. We have no control over the content of these websites or apps, which may change frequently, and we are not responsible for the content or the way it may be used with our materials. Teachers and students are advised to exercise discretion when accessing the links.

The Publisher has made every effort to trace the owner of copyright material; however, the Publisher will correct any involuntary omission at the earliest opportunity.

Printed in Mexico by Editorial Impresora Apolo, S.A. de C.V., Centeno 150-6, Col. Granjas Esmeralda, C.P. 09810, Mexico City.

Contents

Student's Book

- 4 — Scope and Sequence
- 7 — Unit 0 — How do you balance work and fun?
- 13 — Unit 1 — What are you like?
- 27 — Unit 2 — What could I make?
- 41 — Unit 3 — How am I different now?
- 55 — Unit 4 — How green do you want to be?
- 69 — Unit 5 — Is reality stranger than fiction?
- 83 — Unit 6 — What would the world be like if...?
- 97 — Unit 7 — What do I need to live abroad?
- 111 — Unit 8 — What will I do in the future?

Workbook

- 126 — Unit 1
- 130 — Unit 2
- 134 — Unit 3
- 138 — Unit 4
- 142 — Unit 5
- 146 — Unit 6
- 150 — Unit 7
- 154 — Unit 8

- 158 — *Just for Fun* Answer Key
- 159 — Grammar Reference
- 168 — Verb List

Scope and Sequence

Unit	Vocabulary	Grammar	Skills
0 — How do you balance work and fun?	**Review:** air travel, food, household chores, life experiences, music, unusual jobs	Present perfect; Phrasal verbs; Second conditional; Passive voice; Defining and non-defining relative clauses	**Listening:** Listening for specific information
1 — What are you like?	**Personality Traits:** considerate, dishonest, friendly, honest, impatient, inconsiderate, irresponsible, patient, reasonable, responsible, unfriendly, unreasonable	Tag questions	**Reading:** Understanding implicit information **Speaking:** Role-playing a job interview **Project:** Creating a personality quiz
2 — What could I make?	**Materials and Tools:** drill, glue stick, hammer, hot glue gun, nails, plywood, saw, screwdriver, screws, solder, soldering iron	Passive voice (present simple, present continuous, past simple, future, present perfect, modals)	**Listening:** Identifying steps in instructions **Writing:** Writing instructions **Project:** Presenting a life hack
3 — How am I different now?	**Milestones:** attend acting classes, build a drone, create a vlog, develop a computer game, get a part-time job, learn another language, start a band with friends, write a book	Present perfect vs. present perfect continuous	**Reading:** Predicting content **Speaking:** Talking about a life-changing experience **Project:** Creating a vlog
4 — How green do you want to be?	**Sustainable Living:** baking soda, carpool, food leftovers, indoor garden, rechargeable batteries, reusable shopping bags, vinegar	First conditional vs. second conditional	**Listening:** Identifying opinions and facts **Writing:** Writing a report **Project:** Creating an action plan to implement a green initiative at school

Unit	Vocabulary	Grammar	Skills
5 **Is reality stranger than fiction?**	**Strange Creatures and Phenomena:** aliens, clairvoyance, ghosts, telekinesis, telepathy, UFOs, werewolves, zombies	Perfect modals	**Reading:** Reading for main ideas **Writing:** Writing an explanation based on graphic organizers **Project:** Making a presentation about an unsolved mystery
6 **What would the world be like if…?**	**Milestones of the 21st Century:** achieve a breakthrough, break out, disaster, fight a war, go through a crisis, hit, lead a revolution, make a discovery, pandemic	Third conditional; Mixed conditional	**Listening:** Distinguishing facts from opinions **Speaking:** Discussing a historical issue **Project:** Writing a homepage of an online newspaper
7 **What do I need to live abroad?**	**Living Abroad:** apply for a student visa, buy plane tickets, choose a language school, enroll in a course, fill out forms, get a passport, make new friends, make travel arrangements, participate in cultural events, take out travel insurance, try local foods	Reported statements	**Reading:** Reading for specific details **Writing:** Writing a leaflet **Project:** Preparing a section of a guide for foreign college students
8 **What will I do in the future?**	**Future Goals:** be more sympathetic to others, buy a car, buy a house, get married, get a job after college, go to college, have a healthier lifestyle, rent an apartment, save money, start a business, travel the world	Future continuous	**Listening:** Inferring information **Speaking:** Giving a presentation **Project:** Writing an action plan for the future

Unit 0

1 Read the song titles and their artists on the playlist. Match each of them with its genre.

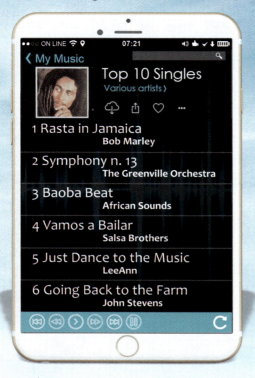

☐ classical ☐ pop
☐ country ☐ reggae
☐ Latin ☐ world music

Guess What!
"See You Again," recorded by rapper Wiz Khalifa and singer Charlie Puth, is one of the most downloaded songs of all times. It sold over 20 million digital copies in 2015.

2 Think Fast! In your notebook, write song titles for these music genres: *country, pop, rap, reggae, rock* and *world music*.

3 Match the verbs to the phrases. Then number the pictures the activities refer to. Two pictures will not be used.

1. camp   your own web page
2. change   in a play
3. design   a boat
4. learn   overnight
5. perform   a horse
6. ride   your look
7. sail   by plane
8. travel   to play a musical instrument

4 Complete the questions in the quiz. Then answer them.

How interested in trying new things are you? Answer and find out!

1. Have you ever gone camping?
2. Have you ever _____ your look?
3. _____ you ever _____ a web page?
4. _____ you ever _____ to play a musical instrument?
5. _____ you ever _____ in a play?
6. _____ you ever _____ a horse?
7. _____ you ever _____ a boat?

5 Work with a partner. Share your answers in Activity 4. Ask for further information.

A: I have already gone camping.
B: Really? Where did you go?
A: I went camping with my uncle in a national park last year. It was great!

Stop and Think! Which of the activities in Activity 3 would you **never** like to do for fun? Why?

6 🎧¹ Rewrite the numbered sentences, replacing the phrases in italics with the corresponding phrasal verb. Then listen and check your answers.

> hang up   pick up   put away   take out   wipe off

DAD: Have you cleaned your room?

SARAH: Yes, I have, Dad. (1) I have *collected my socks from the floor* and (2) I have *placed my clothes on hangers*.

DAD: Good! (3) And have you *cleaned your desk with a cloth*? It was very dusty.

SARAH: Yes, Dad. And I have washed the cloth I used.

DAD: What about the books under your bed? (4) Have you *placed them where you usually keep them*?

SARAH: Of course, Dad. They're on the bookshelf.

DAD: That's great, Sarah. (5) Now could you *remove* the garbage *from the house*, please?

SARAH: But, Dad…

DAD: I don't want to hear any complaints, young lady! Your room was a mess, and you know that everybody needs to help around the house!

1. I have picked up my socks.
2. _____
3. _____
4. _____
5. _____

7 Read the sentences. What happened first? Number 1 and 2.

1. When I arrived at the party, Emma had already left.
   I arrived at the party. ☐   Emma left the party. ☐
2. Alexis had cleaned her room when she went out with her friends.
   Alexis cleaned her room. ☐   Alexis went out with her friends. ☐
3. By the end of the class, Ethan and Dave had finished the test.
   The class finished. ☐   Ethan and Dave finished the test. ☐
4. Andrew had gone home when I got to the mall to meet him.
   Andrew went home. ☐   I got to the mall to meet Andrew. ☐

8 Read the situations below. Write second conditional sentences.

Real Situation:	What People Would Like to Do:
1. I want to go out with my friends, but I have to study.	If I didn't have to study, I would go out with my friends.
2. Kylie wants to go to the movies, but she doesn't have money.	
3. Ann and Jim want to work, but they're too young to get a job.	
4. We'd love to walk to school, but it's far from home.	
5. I don't speak German, so I can't talk to my cousin in Munich.	

9 Complete the diagram with the words in the box.

airport   baggage   boarding pass   customs   destination   flight   luggage   passport   plane

1. First, you book your _____.

2. On the day of the trip, you arrive at the _____.

3. You print out your _____.

4. And then you check in your _____.

5. Next, you go through _____ control.

6. You board the _____.

7. ...and the plane takes off!!!

8. You land at your _____.

9. You go through _____.

10. ...and finally pick up your suitcases at the _____ claim.

10 Complete the sentences with your own ideas. Use *might*, *could*, *may* or *can't*, depending on how possible the sentences are.

1. If I get a part-time job, _____.
2. If I have some free time this weekend, _____.
3. If I don't travel on my next vacation, _____.
4. If my parents allow me to, _____.

Degrees of possibility

− can't ▮▮▮▮ +

can't – not possible
might
could + (not) verb in the base form
may

11 Read the extracts of cooking directions. Do the tasks below.
- Match the extracts to the dishes.
- Underline the verbs for cooking methods.
- Mark (✓) the extracts in the passive voice.

1. Roast the vegetables in a preheated oven (200°C) for 10 minutes. While they are in the oven, you can boil the stock and prepare the skewers. ☐

2. 1 ½ tablespoons of vegetable oil is added to a skillet over high heat. The poultry is fried for 8 minutes or until browned. The garlic, chili pepper and green beans are added. ☐

3. Use a tablespoon to scoop up the dough. Roll into balls and place them on a baking sheet. Bake the balls for 12 minutes or until golden at the edges. ☐

4. The meat and other ingredients are mixed and shaped into patties. They are grilled over charcoal to the desired doneness. ☐

Crunchy Chocolate Chip Cookies

Chicken Kebabs and Vegetable Couscous

Homemade Charcoal Burger

Spicy Turkey with Green Beans

12 In your notebook, rewrite the statements in the passive voice.

1. People consume too much fat in this country.
2. Companies have reduced vacation days for employees.
3. They cleaned the bedrooms and the kitchen yesterday.
4. The cooks are making kebabs with chicken, beef and vegetables.

13 Circle the correct option. Then decide if the sentences are defining (D) or non-defining (ND) relative clauses.

1. A food stylist is a professional **that / which** cooks meals and prepares them to be photographed. ☐
2. Food stylists, **that / who** usually work for food magazines and TV channels, usually make a lot of money. ☐
3. Curling, **that / which** is an Olympic sport, is practiced on ice. ☐
4. It is played with stones **that / which** players slide along the ice to reach a target. ☐

Vocabulary

1 Read the leaflet and circle two words that describe personality traits.

2 Match the sentence halves to create definitions of people's traits.

1. A **responsible** person is able to do what is right and to fulfill...
2. Someone who is **honest** doesn't tell lies.
3. A **friendly** person is cheerful, kind...
4. **Patient** people are able to remain...
5. A **considerate** person thinks about other people's...
6. **Reasonable** people are rational and fair.

☐ feelings and show kindness towards others.
☐ his/her obligations, in a way others can trust him/her.
☐ They are able to think carefully about difficult situations.
☐ calm and not get annoyed when dealing with problems or difficult people.
☐ and helpful. He/she behaves toward other people as if they were friends.
☐ He/she doesn't cheat or steal either.

Guess What!
We use prefixes to form the negative of different adjectives: **im**patient, **in**considerate, **un**reasonable.

3 Think Fast! Name the positive forms of **ir**responsible, **dis**honest and **un**friendly as fast as you can!

30 SECS

Happy Paws Animal Shelter

🔍 We are looking for a responsible and honest teen to be our fundraising volunteer coordinator across town!

Our volunteer will distribute and manage collection cans in stores, where people can donate spare change to Happy Paws.

➕ If you support our cause, are a responsible person and have a few hours free each month, join us!

📱 For more information, send a text message to Steve Porter, **Volunteer Coordinator at Happy Paws:**

555-9543

5 Discuss what personality traits you think Bea and Mike have.

MIKE

BEA

6 🎧² Listen and check your predictions.

7 🎧² Listen again and write what Bea and Mike say, according to how they describe themselves and each other.

Bea: _____
_____

Mike: _____
_____

Stop and Think! What personality traits should volunteers working in different areas have? Why?

15

---

4 Look at the pictures and complete the sentences.

considerate   dishonest   irresponsible   patient   reasonable   unfriendly

1. Alex usually cheats on his exams. He's pretty _____.

2. Mia always comforts her friends when they are in trouble. She's really _____.

3. Alice often helps her little brother with his math homework. She's so _____.

4. Mr. Woo understands we have other subjects and doesn't assign too much homework. He's really _____.

5. Amy and Josh aren't kind or pleasant. Actually, they are very _____.

6. Alyssa usually texts while she's driving. She's kind of _____.

1 Look at the picture and the words below. Make predictions about what is happening.

Bea
resume
experience
fundraising
interviewer
Happy Paws
pets
volunteer work

2 🎧³ Listen and check your predictions. Then choose the correct option to complete the sentences.

1. The people in the picture are…
   - at school. ☐
   - at Happy Paws' office. ☐

2. They are…
   - a teacher and his student. ☐
   - an interviewer and a candidate for a volunteer position. ☐

3 🎧³ Listen again and match each statement to a tag question.

1. This is not your first time at Happy Paws,   a. do you?
2. I see you did volunteer work at Nursing
   Care last year,   b. is it?
3. But you haven't worked there this year,   c. don't you?
4. Their volunteer program was excellent,   d. wasn't it?
5. You like pets,   e. didn't you?
6. But you don't have any fundraising experience,   f. have you?

Tag Questions

Affirmative Statement	Negative Tag
They care for dogs and cats,	don't they?
You are going to do a job interview,	aren't you?

Negative Statement	Affirmative Tag
Bea doesn't have pets,	does she?
Mike is not applying for the position,	is he?

16

4 **Complete with tag questions.**

1. You don't do volunteer work, _____?
2. Bea did well on the interview, _____?
3. Happy Paws will hire only one volunteer, _____?
4. I'm not a very patient person, _____?
5. The interviewer was nice to Bea, _____?
6. You haven't seen the ad on the school board, _____?
7. Mike isn't going to get the position, _____?
8. Bea isn't doing volunteer work at Nursing Care now, _____?

5 🎧4 **Listen and check your answers.**

Intonation in Tag Questions	
When you are **almost sure** about the answer, use **falling intonation**.	You haven't worked at Happy Paws, **have you**? Bea is applying for the job, **isn't she**?
When you are **not sure** about the answer, use **rising intonation**.	You haven't worked at Happy Paws, **have you**? Bea is applying for the job, **isn't she**?

Guess What!
The tag question for *I am* is *aren't I?*
I am brilliant, aren't I?

6 🎧5 **Listen and practice the tag questions.**

7 **Work with a partner. Take turns practicing the tag questions in Activity 4.**

Bea Parker

E-mail: b.parker@woohoo.com
Phone: 555-8451

Personal attributes:
reasonable, friendly, honest, considerate

High school student seeking volunteer position

Education:
Green Lake High School – Currently in Senior Year

Work experience:
Volunteer at Nursing Care, teaching IT classes to older adults

Duration: 12 months

 Pets: None

8 **Think Fast!** Write two other statements followed by tag questions which the interviewer could ask Bea to confirm information from her resume.

Reading and Speaking

1 Read the ad for another position at Happy Paws. Circle T (True) or F (False).

1. The ideal volunteer must like to work with animals with special needs. T F
2. He/she will help during medical procedures with the animals. T F
3. He/she will work at Happy Paws 20 hours a month, on average. T F

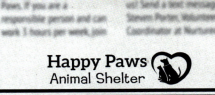

Happy Paws Animal Shelter

Searching for a teen volunteer to work on our team!

Tasks include:
- feeding animals that are sick or unable to eat
- cleaning **kennels**
- assisting vets

If you are a responsible person and can work 3 hours per week, join us! Send a text message to Steven Porter, Volunteer Coordinator at Happy Paws.
555-9543

2 Read the resumes. Write A or K next to the questions below.

Aiden Spencer
a.spencer@coldmail.com
(767) 555-2312

Objective:	High school student seeking volunteer position
Personal attributes:	honest, considerate, responsible
Education:	Green Lake High School – Currently in Senior year
Work experience:	Present – Walk dogs in the neighborhood every afternoon
Language skills:	Fluent Spanish
Achievements:	3rd place in math competition
Pets:	None
Interests:	Member of Green Lake **Choir**, Member of Spanish Club

 Be Strategic!
Find clues and make connections between these clues and your knowledge of the world to understand implicit information in texts.

Kaitlyn Smith
k.smith@woohoo.com
(767) 555-8546

- **Objective:** High school student seeking volunteer position
- **Personal attributes:** patient, friendly, responsible
- **Education:** Green Lake High School – Currently in 11th grade
- **Achievements:** 2nd place in biology competition
- **Pets:** Two dogs and a cat
- **Interests:** Member of Green Lake Animal Care Club, Softball team Captain

Work experience
Present - **Tutor** kids (7 – 10 y.o.) help with their school assignments
Past - Volunteer to feed the sea turtles; cleaned fish tanks at the SeaLife Aquarium

Which candidate…

1. is physically active at work? ☐
2. was a volunteer in the past? ☐
3. works with animals at present? ☐
4. has an interest that is relevant to the position at Happy Paws? ☐

Glossary

kennel: a small place where dogs sleep

choir: an organized group of singers

tutor: to teach an individual student who needs help with schoolwork

 Stop and Think! Do you think it is important to be a volunteer? Why or why not?

3 Mark (✓) the questions an interviewer would ask Aiden and Kaitlyn to get more information about them.

- Why do you want to volunteer for Happy Paws? ☐
- Have you ever traveled abroad? ☐
- Why are you the best candidate for the position? ☐
- What are your expectations for the position? ☐
- How often do you go to the movies? ☐
- You like working with animals, don't you? ☐

4 Complete the phrases used to open and close an interview.

interview   fine   meet   hearing   please   thank   today   touch   welcome   I'm

Opening a Job Interview

Interviewer	Candidate
_____ to Happy Paws. _____ Steven Porter. Nice to meet you. _____ have a seat.	_____ you. I'm glad to be here. Nice to _____ you too. I'm _____, thanks.

Closing a Job Interview

Interviewer	Candidate
Thank you for coming _____. I'll be in _____ soon.	Thanks for the _____. I look forward to _____ from you!

5 Choose one of the roles below and role-play a job interview. Then switch roles.

Interviewer: Steven Porter
You are going to interview Aiden or Kaitlyn. Read Aiden and Kaitlyn's resumes again.

Candidate: Aiden or Kaitlyn
Read Aiden or Kaitlyn's resumes again. Be ready to answer Steven Porter's questions.

Culture

1 Label the pictures of the animals.

mountain lion   mole   eagle   wolf   coyote   bear   badger

2 Complete the first column of the chart according to your associations between the animals and the words.

Key Words	My Association	Zuni People Beliefs
	Animal	Animal
1. **aware**, introspective		
2. dominant, **resourceful**		
3. creative, intuitive		
4. strong, introspective		
5. aggressive, perseverant		
6. loyal, **wise**		
7. good - humored, foolish		

3 Read and compare the information with your ideas in Activity 2. Complete the second column of the chart.

Fetishes and ◈ Zuni ◈ People

Fetishes are small objects that depict animals or icons that are important in several North American indigenous cultures. They are **carved** in stone, precious gems, coral, shells and other materials. North American Indians believe that fetishes have magical powers and give people protection at different moments in life. Nowadays, these hand-carved figures are considered to be pieces of artwork. Among the different fetishes made by various indigenous peoples, the ones created by the Zuni people are the most admired.

The Zuni tribe lives in New Mexico, in the United States, where they keep a set of traditional customs – and carving fetishes is one of them. They make fetishes of animals whose characteristics are important to them.

Mountain lion – Seen as having leadership skills and as being resourceful and powerful.

Bear – Associated with strength, introspection and self-knowledge. Also seen as the great protector and healer.

Coyote – Respected for its survival skills and related to humor and the ability to laugh at oneself.

Badger – Although seen as aggressive, perseverance is the main characteristic of this animal according to the Zuni people.

Eagle – Known for its creativity, intuition and great vision. Also seen as a healer.

Mole – Considered protector of crops and the underground. The Zuni people see it as a symbol of introspection and awareness.

Wolf – Since this animal always lives in **packs**, it's seen as an example of loyalty and wisdom and an advocate of family values.

4 Complete the mind map about the Zuni people.

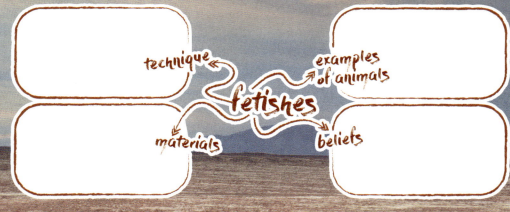

5 🎧⁶ Listen and match each person to the fetish they have.

1. Allison
2. Keith
3. Joanna

Stop and Think! Are there any animals associated with personality traits in your culture?

Glossary

aware: showing understanding of things around you

resourceful: good at solving problems

wise: showing great knowledge from experience

carve: to make something by cutting off pieces of a material

pack: a group of predatory animals

Project

1 Look at the text below and mark (✓) the text type.

☐ a quiz ☐ an interview

How Responsible Are You?

1 You've been playing video games for hours, but you need to study for a test. What do you do?

a) You keep playing the game. You don't want to study after all. ☐
b) You keep playing the game, but you worry about the test. ☐
c) You stop playing right away and get to your notes. ☐

2 Your parents have an important appointment in the evening. If they go, they will get back home in the middle of the night. What do you do?

a) You show empathy so they don't worry about you. You will then secretly throw a party while they are out. ☐
b) You tell them you need someone to make dinner for you. After all, you can't even make a sandwich. ☐
c) You say they can go and promise you will call them once or twice to say how things are going. ☐

3 Some friends decide to skip classes to hang out at a park and invite you to join them. What do you do?

a) You join them. After all, having fun is the best thing in life! ☐
b) You go with them, but you're so afraid of getting caught that you don't have any fun. ☐
c) You decide not to go and feel OK about it. You can hang out on the weekend. ☐

4 You want to buy a new bike, but your parents say they can't afford it. What do you do?

a) You cry and bother your parents until they change their minds. ☐
b) You get really sad and complain about your parents to a friend. ☐
c) You get a part-time job to save money for the bike. ☐

5 Your parents give you a prepaid cell phone. How do you use it?

a) You always ask your parents to add credit to it before the end of the month. ☐
b) Sometimes you run out of credit, but most of the time you can control its use. ☐
c) You never run out of credit. You're able to manage the account well. ☐

Most a answers –
You aren't worried about being responsible—in fact, most people would say you're irresponsible. It's important to start thinking about your actions and their consequences.

Most b answers –
You're not a very responsible person, but it's clear that you worry about the consequences of your actions. Try to think before acting—this will help you do better in life.

Most c answers –
Congrats! You're a responsible teenager! You're able to stay out of trouble and know how to balance hard work and fun. Keep it up!

2 Circle *T* (True) or *F* (False).
1. The quiz is divided into numbered questions.   T   F
2. It offers different possible answers.   T   F
3. There is one correct answer for each question.   T   F
4. The questions and answers are about personal experiences.   T   F

3 Work in small groups to create and carry out a quiz.

Step 1: Choose a positive personality trait to complete the title of your quiz.

How _____ are you?

considerate   **honest**   *reasonable*

friendly   **patient**

Step 2: Write five questions and possible answers, according to the personality trait in Step 1. Use your personal experience to come up with realistic situations.

Step 3: Write possible answers to each question. Plan them in such a way that they clearly represent the personality trait. Look at the quiz on page 22 and use the diagram below to help you plan the answers.

a   b   c

irresponsible   kind of responsible   responsible

Step 4: When the questions and answers are ready, write the results. Look at the example of the quiz on page 22.

4 Now exchange your quiz with another group. Have them answer your questions while you work on their quiz. Good luck!

Review

1 Complete the chart.

Personality Traits	
Positive	Negative
considerate	
friendly	
	dishonest
patient	
	unreasonable
	irresponsible

2 Look at the scenes. Use adjectives from Activity 1 to describe the people in them.

How Would You Describe These People?				
Young Man in Scene 1	Teen Girl in Scene 2	Street Vendor in Scene 3	Teen Boy in Scene 4	People in Line in Scene 5

3 Circle the correct pronoun.

1. That animal shelter helps dogs find new homes, doesn't **it / he**?
2. Alex and Thomas are very responsible guys, aren't **we / they**?
3. Mrs. Taylor is our most patient teacher, isn't **she / he**?
4. You and I haven't been here before, have **we / I**?
5. Those children are really friendly, aren't **you / they**?
6. I was a considerate friend during your sickness, wasn't **you / I**?

4 Match the sentences to the tag questions.

Steven Porter
1. … works as a volunteer at Happy Paws,
2. … isn't the fundraising coordinator,

Bea Parker
3. … wrote in her resume that she is friendly,
4. … wasn't a volunteer at Kids4Life,

Aiden Spencer
5. … has learned Spanish,
6. … doesn't have pets,

Kaitlyn Smith
7. … will be a senior next year,
8. … plays softball at school,

- was she?
- does he?
- doesn't she?
- didn't she?
- won't she?
- is he?
- doesn't he?
- hasn't he?

5 Write tag questions.

1. Steven interviewed Bea, Aiden and Kaitlyn, _____?
2. He will hire the best candidate, _____?
3. Bea studies at Blue Lake High School, _____?
4. She didn't work at Happy Paws last year, _____?
5. Aiden is in his senior year in high school, _____?
6. He doesn't walk dogs in the morning, _____?
7. Kaitlyn has been a volunteer at Sea Life, _____?
8. She was second in a competition in her school, _____?

Just for Fun

1 Complete the crossword puzzle with the opposite form of the adjectives.

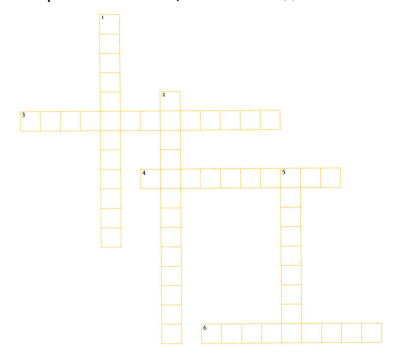

Down
1. reasonable
2. considerate
5. honest

Across
3. responsible
4. friendly
6. patient

2 Write four animals from the Culture section in the grid. Then play battleship with a classmate.

3 Play tic-tac-toe with a classmate. Create sentences with the tag questions.

did you?	won't they?	does she?
has it?	**Choose the tag!**	is it?
don't we?	wasn't he?	are you?

1 Look at the items below. Organize them in the chart.

> 28

SOME THINGS YOU NEED TO START IN DIY

DIY (or Do It Yourself) is the activity of making, repairing or recycling things at home, instead of buying them, or having professional assistance to do them.

solder / soldering iron

screwdriver / screws

glue stick / hot glue gun

hammer / nails

drill

plywood / saw

May • Stopwatch Magazine •123

Tools	Materials

2 🎧⁷ **Now listen and check your answers.**

3 **Read the sentences and write the item from Activity 1 each one refers to.**

1. This tool, when heated, is used to melt solder and join metal parts: _____
2. This material has a sharp end and it is used to fix one piece of wood to another: _____
3. This tool is used, with electricity, to make holes in hard surfaces: _____
4. This tool is used to cut wood. There is a version of it powered by electricity: _____
5. This material is solid, but when melted by heat, it is used to stick things: _____
6. This material is a board made of layers or wood and it is used to build furniture: _____

4 **Look at the items below. Which tools and materials from Activity 1 are used to make them? Write them in your notebook.**

A beetle bot   A bookcase

5 🎧⁸ **Listen to Sarah and Matt talking about a DIY project. Circle the tools they mention.**

6 🎧⁸ **Listen again and complete the list. Then say which item from Activity 4 Sarah and Matt are planning to make.**

Materials:
> Six boards of _____
> A pack of _____
> Five _____

Guess What! According to safety rules, people must:
WEAR GLOVES   WEAR GOGGLES   WEAR HELMET

Stop and Think! What are some advantages and disadvantages of recycling and DIY?

1 Read the texts. Which invention is the oldest?

Inventions
FLYING MACHINES

9 Facts about Amazing Flying Machines

From DIY devices to big spacecrafts!

1. The inventor Nikola Tesla is called "The father of UAV technology." He invented the first remote control system in 1898.

2. **Drones** are also known as Unmanned Aerial Vehicles (UAVs). They were developed after World War II and have been used by military forces since then. Nowadays, drone DIY kits are sold on the internet so that people can build their own UAVs at home.

3. For civilians, the most popular drone model is the quadcopter. It can even be built at home!

4. Drones with cameras are being used by TV channels to fly over areas of news stories, such as natural disasters.

Did you know? In the future, drones will be used by Amazon, the e-commerce company, to deliver packages to customers.

5. **SpaceShipTwo (SS2)** will be the first spacecraft for space tourism. It is being developed by Virgin Galactic, a spaceflight company.

6. Virgin Galactic was founded by Sir Richard Branson, one of the richest men in the world.

7. In its suborbital flights, six passengers will be carried by SS2. Each flight will last about 2.5 hours.

8. According to Virgin Galactic plans, lack of gravity will be experienced by passengers for six minutes during the flight.

9. Burt Rutan, one of the main designers of SS2, designed and built his own prototype planes in his garage in the 1960s.

Did you know? Over 700 tickets have been sold for future suborbital flights. Each ticket cost US$ 250,000!

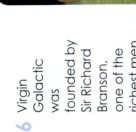

2 Underline the passive voice forms in the text.

3 Read the headlines. Write A if the verb is in the active form, or P if it is in the passive form.

Quadcopter Crash Near Greenville School; Nobody Was Injured ☐

NASA Announces Partnership with Virgin Galactic ☐

Why Nikola Tesla Was Forgotten by History ☐

I Was Given Free Tickets for SpaceShip Two!" says Stephen Hawking ☐

AMAZON REVEALS PLANS FOR DELIVERY DRONE ☐

Amazing Tweets: Sir Richard Branson Has Over 7 Million Followers on Twitter ☐

Active Voice vs. Passive Voice

Active Voice
TV channels *are using* drones with cameras.
Agent / Subject — Verb — Object

Passive Voice
Drones with cameras *are being used by* TV channels.
Subject — form of *be* + past participle — Agent

4 Complete the sentences with the passive form of the verbs.

1. Some great inventions and product innovations _____ by people during their leisure time. (*make* – simple present)
2. Many DIY fans _____ at makerspaces—specially designed places that provide tools and materials for people who want to build things. (*can/find*)
3. Nowadays, drones _____ by the American government to protect wildlife. (*use* – present continuous)
4. An aircraft to launch small satellites _____ by Virgin Galactic. (*develop* – present perfect)
5. According to NASA, a human mission _____ to Mars in the mid-2030s. (*send* – future with *will*)

5 Match the items in the columns to write sentences in the passive voice in your notebook.

1. Apple	start	to surf the Internet by millions of people nowadays.
2. Smartphones	use	in the first half of the 20th century.
3. Helicopters	invent	by Tim Berners-Lee in 1989. He also invented the web browser.
4. The World Wide Web	develop	by Steve Jobs, Steve Wozniak and Ronald Wayne in 1976.

6 Think Fast! Work with a partner. Write two newspaper headlines in the passive voice, similar to the ones in Activity 3.

3 min

Listening and Writing

1 **Do you know what a hack is? Read the definition and find out.**

> **Hack (Noun):** a creative and efficient solution to a limitation of a product, a computer program or any other object.

2 **Look at the hack below and discuss with a classmate what kind of problem it solves.**

3 🎧⁹ **Listen and confirm your guess in Activity 2.**

4 🎧¹⁰ **Order the steps to make the hack. Then listen and check your answers.**

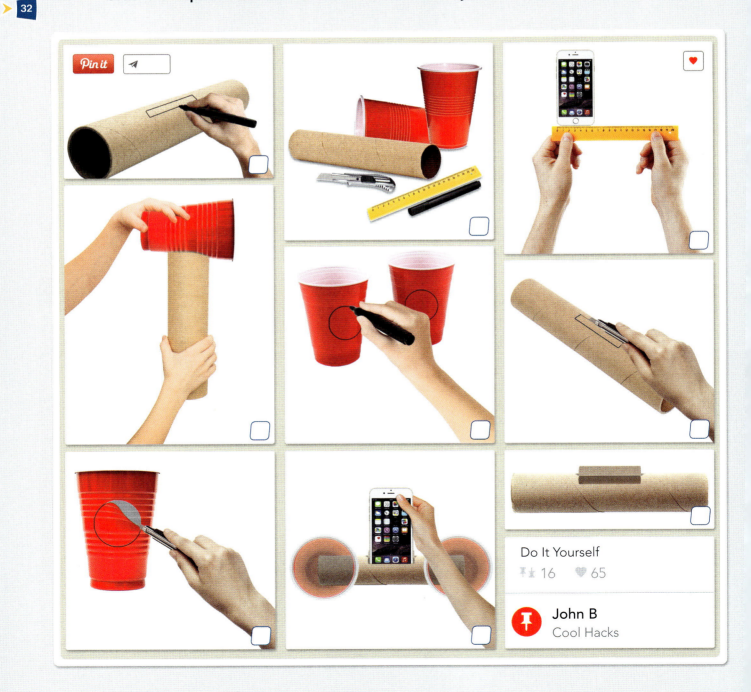

Do It Yourself

John B
Cool Hacks

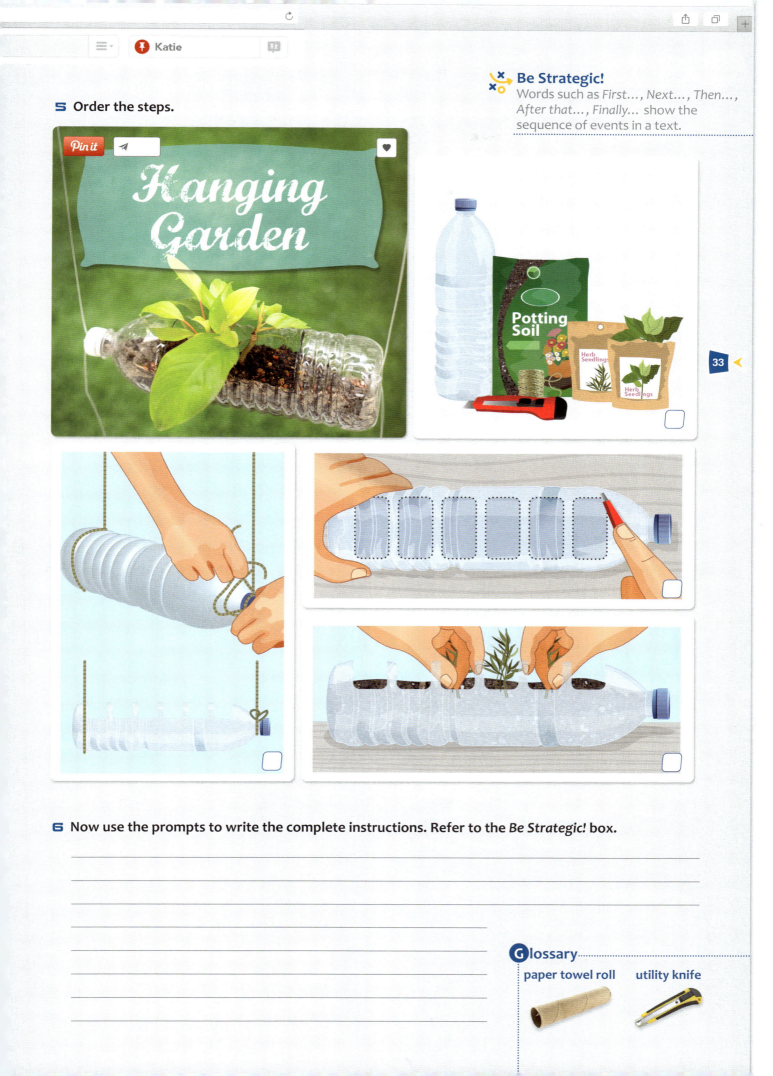

Culture

1. Look at the pictures. Discuss with a classmate how you think they are related to Kelvin Doe, a young inventor.

Guess What!
Sierra Leone is a small country located in the western part of Africa, between Guinea, Liberia and the Atlantic Ocean. It has over 6 million inhabitants and its capital is Freetown. Lack of jobs is a serious problem, mainly among young people.

Stop and Think! Do you know any young person in your country who came up with simple and cheap solutions for everyday problems?

2 Now read a fact sheet about Kelvin. Order the paragraphs in the text.

Biography

POLITICS ENTERTAINMENT INVENTS WORLD NEWS

Kelvin Doe, a.k.a. DJ Focus

Date of birth: October 26, 1996
Home country: Sierra Leone, in Africa
Occupation: Student and DJ

But this problem actually became a source of inspiration for the young Sierra Leonean. He used soda, acid, metal, tape and a tin cup to make his own battery. One year later, he used objects found around his house and others picked from the garbage to build a generator. ☐

When Kelvin was 13 years old, he learned engineering and electronics by himself. However, electricity was scarce in his neighborhood, and he didn't have either the resources to power his creations or the money to buy batteries. ☐

Now back to Sierra Leone, Kelvin continues to pursue his interests in electronics and engineering. He is also a champion for all young innovators in his country and on the African continent. ☐

Besides powering his house and neighbors' cell phones, Kelvin's generator made one of his dreams possible: in that same year, he created a homemade radio station and became a DJ! ☐

Kelvin's accomplishments took him to winning an innovation award for high school students in Sierra Leone. After that, he was invited to visit MIT in 2012, and to speak at TEDxTeen in New York the following year. Since then, he has participated in several events in his country and around the world. ☐

"I believe that through innovation, we can build our nation Sierra Leone."
Kelvin Doe

---

3 Were your ideas about Kelvin in Activity 1 right? Read the biography again, if necessary.

4 Write the milestones in Kelvin's life in the appropriate place on his timeline.

1. Visited the Massachusetts Institute of Technology
2. Was born in Freetown, Sierra Leone
3. Spoke to an audience in New York
4. Built his own batteries
5. Is encouraging other teenagers in Sierra Leone to innovate
6. Built his own generator and created a radio station

1996 — 2009 — 2010 — 2012 — 2013 — Now

1 Read this text about life hacking. Did you know about these life hack ideas?

What the Heck Is Life Hacking After All?

HOW TO KNOW IF AN EGG IS STILL FRESH

USE A PEN SPRING TO PREVENT YOUR CHARGER FROM BREAKING

Imagine this situation: Melissa wants to have eggs for breakfast, but she's not sure if the eggs in her fridge are good to eat, or if they have gone bad. She knows that cracking bad eggs is an awful experience, and the kitchen would smell of rotten eggs for hours if she did it.

Then she remembers her grandma once said there's a simple test to check if eggs are still good. Melissa fills a glass with cold water and places an egg in it. If the egg sinks, it means it's still fresh; if it floats, it means it's rotten. She has three good eggs and happily makes her breakfast.

The imaginary situation we described is an example of life hacking—a way of dealing with problems by finding tricks or shortcuts to save time, increase efficiency or simply to make life easier.

Tech journalist Danny O'Brien first came up with the term *life hack* at a conference in San Diego, California, in 2004. He used it to describe mini-programs that were created by IT professionals to make their work easier. Since then, life hacking has been used to describe any creative strategies or techniques adopted to solve problems or to increase productivity—either old ones, like Melissa's grandma's trick with the eggs, or new ones, like using a pen spring to prevent your cell phone charger from breaking.

2 Work in small groups and come up with a life hack. Follow the steps below.

Steps

1 Think of a problem you or your friends (or people you know) face every day.
Tip! Don't worry about big problems, such as climate change—think of those small, repeated problems that annoy you all the time.

2 Discuss with your classmates why this issue is a problem and if it can be solved somehow.
Tip! Some problems simply don't have a solution. If it rains in your city every afternoon and you hate it, you'd better move to a drier place whenever you can.

3 Now discuss some possible solutions. You can use a large sheet of paper to brainstorm ideas.
Tip! Check some suggestions to come up with a hack:
- Search the Internet—use keywords related to the issue.
- Browse books and magazines related to the topic of your problem.
- Look at everyday objects in your schoolbag and around your house—can they have other creative uses to solve your problem?
- Write down any ideas you have. If something comes up while you are riding your bike to school, for example, use your smartphone to record the idea.
- Try to meet your classmates to brainstorm ideas in a different place, outside school, such as a café or a park. Simply changing location can boost creativity!

4 Once you have your life hack—or a plan to create it—prepare a presentation to share it with the other groups. You can use the chart below to organize your presentation in your notebook.

Problem	Why Did It Bother Us?	Life Hack	Materials and Tools	Instructions

3 Now present your life hack to the class.

Stop and Think! Which life hack was the most interesting? Why?

1 **Which tools are these? Look and label.**

2 **Label the pictures. Then complete the chart with the tools in Activity 1 the materials are commonly used with.**

Material					
Tool					

3 **Correct the mistakes in the sentences.**

1. Let's find a drill to knock these nails into the plywood.
   _____

2. Can you get me a screwdriver? I want to remove this solder.
   _____

3. I'm going to the office supply store downtown. I need to buy nails for my hot glue gun.
   _____

4. Emily wants to use a saw to make a hole in the wall, but she has never done it.
   _____

4 **Which materials or tools have you already worked with? Write two examples in your notebook. Say what you used them for.**

5 Are these sentences in the active or passive voice? In the passive sentences, circle the agent, if it is mentioned.

	Active	Passive
1. Steve Jobs founded Apple Computers in 1976, in his parents' garage.		
2. The first cell phone call was made by Martin Cooper on April 3, 1973.		
3. Water talkies are used by swimmers to communicate under water. They were invented by a 10-year-old boy in 1995.		
4. Kelly knows how to make a purse out of pull rings from cans.		

6 Transform the active sentences into passive ones.

1. My mom recycled a lamp bulb to make this vase.
   A lamp bulb _____ by my mother to make this vase.
2. Brazilian mechanic Alfredo Moser used a bottle of water with bleach to light up a room in his house. People call his invention the "Moser Lamp."
   A bottle of water with bleach _____ by Brazilian mechanic Alfredo Moser to light up a room in his house. The invention _____ the "Moser Lamp."
3. Did Bill Gates found Microsoft?
   _____ by Bill Gates?
4. In the future, pizza places will use drones to deliver pizza to customers' houses.
   In the future, _____ by pizza places to deliver pizza to customers' houses.

7 Complete the sentences with the passive voice of the verbs. Then match the sentences to the pictures they describe.

1. This device _____ (invent) by Alexander Graham Bell in 1876. Nowadays, its mobile version is very popular among people all ages.
2. This device _____ (sell) to millions of people since it became popular, in the 1940s. Nowadays, most people have at least one of them at home.
3. This monument _____ (design) by the French as a gift to the country where it _____ (locate), at the end of the 19th century.
4. This monument _____ (create) by a French sculptor.
   It _____ (make) of concrete and soapstone.

Christ the Redeemer

The telephone

The Statue of Liberty

The TV set

Just for Fun

1 Use the clues to guess the words.

40

2 Find the names of the items in the mirrored word search.

```
R B P L L I R D K R K V O K A
K S T R R V N O E W E H W C I
U U P C B W C O W P S D X X L
P T Z T W B V W R X J H L K U
Q X L Q J F W Y C K M G U O V
S W E R C S B L K D J Z T D S
P M W V M M K P P E P V M J K
N O R I G N I R E D L O S I D
V M A H S I A R H O V V O S C
Z Q G L O R A K X U U Z E U W
```

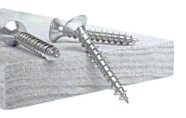  

3 Create a quote with the letters below.

		D	A		I	L	E		F		J		N	K	
A	N	O		I	N	P	I	M	A		I	Y	A	U	I	N	E
A	T	G	O	O	D	V	E	N	T	G	O	N	O	T	U	O	N	E	D

"	T	O		I	N	V	E	N	T	,									
													J	U	N	K	.	"	

> Thomas Edison, American inventor

Vocabulary

1 Complete the captions with the words from the box.

> abroad   alone   acting classes
> band with your friends   book
> computer game   drone   vlog
> foreign language   part-time job

This Month's Feature:
Activities that Can Change Your Life!

Tired of your home-school-home routine? Our readers suggest things you can do to break your routine, spice up your life and acquire valuable skills and experience for your future!

"Develop your own _____"

– Zach, 15

"Learn a _____"

– Hailey, 16

"Write a _____"

– Matt, 15

"Travel _____"

– Emma, 16

"Attend _____"

– Jasmine, 15

"Get a _____"

– Katie, 16

"Start a _____"

– Tyler and Olivia, 16

Guess What!
Christopher Paolini is the youngest best-selling author in the world! He started the Inheritance Cycle with the book *Eragon* when he was 15 years old!

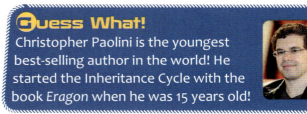

83 • STOPWATCH MAGAZINE

"Create a _____" "Build your own _____"

– Dylan, 14

– Alyssa, 15

2. 🎧¹⁰ **Listen to a presentation of the results of a survey. Match the colors with the activities.**

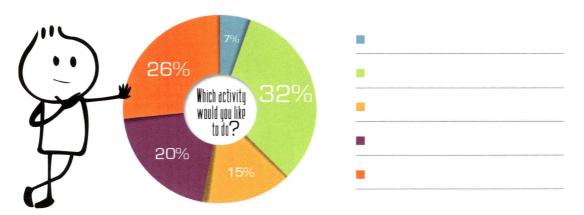

3. **Complete the chart with the activities on page 42.**

I have done it!	I haven't done it, but would like to.	I haven't done it, and wouldn't like to.

4. **Now share your ideas from Activity 3 with a friend. Explain your choices.**

 Stop and Think! Which of the activities in this lesson would have the most impact on a teenager's future? Why?

1 Read the blog posts. Which activities from the Vocabulary section do they refer to?

Blog post 1: _____ Blog post 2: _____

The Travel Lover Blog

Posted by: Julia Stevenson
Wednesday March 2, 12:08 p.m.

PIAZZA SAN MARCO, EARLIER TODAY

I have been touring around Italy for two weeks now. I miss my parents and little sister, but I've been enjoying this adventure by myself!

I have been visiting different cities by train, most of the time—the views from the train window are breathtaking.

I'm in Venice now. I've seen Piazza San Marco and the Bridge of Sighs, but there's a lot more to see this afternoon.

It's lunch time now. I've been eating A LOT of Italian food since I arrived here—it's simply delicious! Tomorrow evening I'll take another train to Milan, but I haven't packed yet, of course!

Check my photo social network profile (TravelLover17) for all the pictures I've taken in Venice and in other places in Italy.

That's all for now!

1 comment

- About
- Destination
- Places to visit
- Travel tips
- Follow me on

The Young Job Seeker

Posted by: Tyler Smith
Wednesday, March 2 – 3:16 p.m.

Hi guys! I've done so much already to reach my goal, but things haven't been easy—actually, they've been much more difficult than I've imagined…

I've written a nice resume and have sent it to some job vacancies in my town. I've only had one job interview so far, and I don't think I did well. =(

Since then, I've been practicing job interview questions with my friend Alice. She's great! She's been working at a local ice cream parlor for six months now, and had several interviews before getting this job—she's a pro when it comes to job interviews. =D

Alice has also given me advice on how to look for a job. I've been checking job ads on the Internet for some days now – there are many more opportunities online than in newspapers! I hope I'll be working like Alice quite soon!

1 comment

► Alice at work.

2 Underline the present perfect form and circle the present perfect continuous form in the blog posts.

Present Perfect vs. Present Perfect Continuous

I've seen Piazza San Marco and the Bridge of Sighs. (finished action; when ➝ ???)
I've been touring Italy for two weeks. (action in progress; started in the past)

Julia has been eating Italian food *since* she arrived in Italy. (moment in time)
for two weeks. (period of time)

3 Complete the sentences. Use the present perfect continuous.

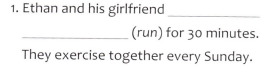

1. Ethan and his girlfriend _____ _____ (run) for 30 minutes. They exercise together every Sunday.

2. Jake _____ (learn) French since he came back from Paris last March.

3. Lauren _____ (record) videos for her vlog for a year. She's a famous vlogger now.

4. Some of my classmates _____ _____ (attend) acting classes since the beginning of the school year. They really enjoy acting!

4 🎧12 Listen to four conversations. Are the actions finished, or are they still in progress?

1. Savannah – build a drone
   finished ☐   in progress ☐
2. Logan – write a book
   finished ☐   in progress ☐
3. Julia – travel
   finished ☐   in progress ☐
4. Sean – play with his band
   finished ☐   in progress ☐

5 Complete the sentences with the present perfect or the present perfect continuous.

1. My English is really good now. I have _____. (study)
2. The chocolate cake is ready now! It has _____. (finish baking)
3. You play the guitar pretty well! How long _____? (practice)
4. Do you know where my keys are? I _____ (see – neg.)

6 Think Fast! Write a comment for each blog post in Activity 1.

Reading and Speaking

12

1. Read the title of the article and its lead. Then look at the photos and the map. What do you think it is about?

 Be Strategic!
Predicting content helps you understand any text better. Always read the title, look at photos and analyze any other visuals before reading. Ask yourself, "What does this information tell me about the text I'm going to read?"

2. Now read the article to check your predictions in Activity 1.

Laura Dekker
A Young Adventurer

Her greatest feat—being the youngest person to circumnavigate the planet—made her internationally famous. But Laura Dekker's passion for the sea and for adventure started much earlier than people imagine.

• She was only 14 when she went on a journey that changed her life—all by herself.

Born in New Zealand in 1995, Laura has been involved with the sea since her mom's belly—actually, her parents were on a long sailing journey around the world when she was born. Her family only returned to their home country, Holland, when she was five.

In Holland, Laura began to nurture a love for sailing. At the age of six, she sailed alone for the first time and has been participating in sailing competitions since then. Four years later, she bought her first boat, using money saved from doing jobs and chores, and sailed it around the North Sea and Holland. In 2009, she sailed from Holland to England all by herself.

The idea of solo circumnavigation came up after the trip to England. When she was getting ready for the challenging journey, the Dutch government claimed she was too young to do it. Laura and her father went to court, and in July, 2010, she won the right to make the trip.

Her journey started on August 21, 2010. She departed from **Gibraltar**, a British territory in the south of Spain, on her new boat *Guppy*.

3. Read the article again. Mark (✓) YES, NO or NOT MENTIONED for the statements below.

	YES	NO	NOT MENTIONED
1. Laura Dekker is the youngest person to sail around the world by herself.	☐	☐	☐
2. She bought her first boat when she was 12 years old.	☐	☐	☐
3. Guppy was the boat Laura used to sail from Holland to England.	☐	☐	☐
4. The governments of several countries were against her solo journey.	☐	☐	☐
5. Laura's solo circumnavigation lasted 17 months.	☐	☐	☐
6. Laura visited one of the places twice in her journey.	☐	☐	☐

CURRENT NEWSPAPER
Sunday, March 25

13

Main stops and milestones in her solo circumnavigation:
- **December 2, 2010:** Crossed the Atlantic, from Cape Verde to Saint Martin, in the Caribbean
- **April 11, 2011:** Crossed the Panama Canal, reaching the Pacific Ocean
- **April 26, 2011:** Arrived in the Galapagos Islands, on the coast of South America
- **July, 2011:** Visited several islands in Tahiti
- **August 25, 2011:** Reached Darwin, in Australia, crossing the Pacific Ocean
- **November 12, 2011:** Crossed the Indian Ocean, arriving in Durban, South Africa
- **January 21, 2012:** Completed her journey going back to Saint Martin. This was the longest leg of the circumnavigation, with 10,400 km.

4 How do you think Laura's life changed after her solo sailing? Discuss with a partner.

5 🎧13 Now listen to a conversation about another life-changing experience. Then circle *T* (True) or *F* (False).
1. Matt had leukemia.   T   F
2. He started his own company.   T   F
3. He started running marathons.   T   F

6 🎧13 Listen again. Then match the questions from the conversations to their meaning.
1. How long have you been running marathons?
2. Why did you start?
3. Did you run a marathon before that?
4. How has running marathons changed your life?

☐ Find out reasons for starting the activity.
☐ Check whether a piece of information is true.
☐ Verify the amount of time the person has performed the activity.
☐ Find out the way the activity has affected the person.

7 Take notes in your notebook about a life-changing experience. You can also imagine one. Use the chart below.

Experience:	
When:	
Why:	
Change in your life:	

8 Now take turns sharing the experience with a classmate. Use the questions in Activity 6.

47

Culture

1 How much do you know about the 2004 Indian Ocean tsunami? Write key words in the chart below. You can look at the pictures for some ideas.

When?	Where?	Why?	Other Information

A second **tidal wave** in Phuket, Thailand, during the 2004 tsunami

Partially destroyed by the tsunami, this ship landed over 1km away from the coast

Italian restaurant destroyed by the 2004 tsunami

TSUNAMI HAZARD ZONE

2 Read the information below and confirm your guesses.

On December 26, 2004, one of the worst natural disasters ever registered struck several countries in Southeast Asia. It all started with a huge **earthquake** (whose magnitude was between 9.1 and 9.3), which hit the bottom of the Indian Ocean on the coast of Indonesia. It triggered massive tsunamis —also known as tidal waves— which devastated coastal areas in many countries: Indonesia, Thailand, Sri Lanka, Malaysia and India, among others.

Tsunami zone sign in Thai and in English

Guess What!
Phuket Island is a famous vacation spot on the west coast of Thailand. Its main city is Patong, where several resorts attract thousands of tourists every year.

☐ ☐ ☐ ☐ ☐

3 🎧¹⁴ Listen to a podcast and mark (✓) the sentences that are true.

1. Tilly Smith has been living with her family in Phuket Island, in Thailand, for ten years.
2. Tilly was walking on the beach when she noticed there was something strange on the sea.
3. A geography class helped Tilly understand what was happening on the beach.
4. Tilly's mother was the first person who believed in what she was saying.
5. The hotel security guard ignored Tilly's words and didn't warn the tourists on the beach.
6. A tsunami wave hit the beach and Tilly's hotel, but fortunately, there were no deaths.

4 🎧¹⁴ Rewrite the false statements so that they are correct. Then listen again to check.

_____
_____
_____
_____

5 Why is Tilly Smith's story a remarkable life-changing experience? Discuss with a partner.

Stop and Think! Are there any policies to help people cope with natural disasters in your country? Do you know what to do in case of a natural disaster?

lossary
tidal wave: a high wave in the sea, created by an earthquake or strong winds
earthquake: a sudden shaking in the Earth's surface
froth: bubbles of foam that form on the top of the waves

▶ 49

Project

1 How much do you know about vlogs? Use the words below to talk about them with a classmate.

- Video blog
- Vloggers and YouTubers
- Anonymous people → celebrities
- Fast-paced videos
- Simple production—usually only one camera

2 Read the definition. Is there any new information about it that you didn't know?

Vlog [*noun*]

A video weblog hosted on a video sharing platform on the Internet. People who create vlogs—called **vloggers**—usually share personal stories and/or opinions, or a skill that they are good at, with viewers.

Vlogs have become very popular on YouTube and some vloggers are local and international celebrities.

3 Are there any vlogs you often follow or you would like to follow? Complete the chart below.

Vlog Title	Vlogger's Name	Topic	Why I Like It	What I Learn from It

4 Work in small groups. Share your ideas in Activity 3.

5 Work in the same groups of Activity 4. You will create a vlog post. Follow the steps below.

Steps

1 Think of a topic you and the classmates in your group would like to discuss, or a skill one of you is good at—this will be the theme of your vlog post.
Tip! Consider your audience—in this case, your classmates—in order to choose a topic.

2 Discuss the tasks each of you will be responsible for. Some of the roles when recording a vlog post are:
> **Vlogger** – this person should be an extrovert and feel comfortable in front of a camera.
> **Producer** – the person in charge of finding the props or any other materials necessary for recording and arranging the set.
> **Videographer** – the person responsible for recording the video.
> **Editor** – the person who will edit the recording later.

3 Decide if you are going to write a script, or improvise the vlog post.
Tip! Popular vloggers give the impression they are improvising, but they actually rehearse their script to make it sound natural.

4 Collect all the props you need. Use a cell phone, a tablet or a digital camera to record the vlog post
Tip! It is important to use a device with a *good quality* camera.

5 Is everything ready? Record the vlog post. Don't worry if you need to record it again and again.

6 Edit the vlog post, if necessary.
Tip! You can add special effects, stickers and frames to your video to make it more interesting!

 Stop and Think! Did you learn something new from your classmates? How can the activities in this section impact your life?

6 Now present your vlog post to your classmates.

00:00:00:14

Review

1 Look at some objects that different people put together. What are they going to do? Complete the sentences.

> attend acting classes   build a drone   create a vlog   develop a computer game   get a part-time job
> learn a foreign language   start a band with friends   travel abroad alone   write a book

Chloe is trying to _____
_____

Connor wants to start to _____
_____, but he's out of ideas.

Elijah is ready to _____
_____, but his parents are kind of worried.

Hunter got a new computer in order to _____
_____

Kylie will use her smartphone to _____
_____

Becky is writing flashcards to help her _____
_____

Nick and Julia are working hard to _____

Rachel plans to _____
_____

Austin will start to _____
_____

2 What are these people doing? Read the short conversations and find out.

1. Melissa: Do you think it will fly?

   Julia: Of course it will! We just need to follow the instructions on the kit.

   Melissa and Julia are _____

2. Kyle: I play the guitar pretty well, but I don't sing.

   Elijah: We need to find a lead singer, then. Let's talk to Gabriella.

   Kyle and Elijah are _____

3 Complete the sentences with the present perfect continuous.

1. Do you know how long Morgan _____ (look) for a job?
2. The counselor _____ (help) us apply to universities since the beginning of the year.
3. _____ (you – wait) for the interview for a long time?
4. Aidan and I _____ (attend – neg) French classes for a week now. Our teacher is sick.
5. My grandpa _____ (write) a book about the history of our family.

4 Circle the correct word.

1. Thomas and I have been playing together in the school band **for / since** we were in 6th grade.
2. Have you been attending acting classes **for / since** you moved here?
3. People have been flying drones for fun **for / since** a decade now.

5 Decide if the sentences are Right (R) or Wrong (W). Correct the wrong sentences.

1. Lukas has been getting a part-time job as a waiter in a café. He's very happy. ☐
   _____
2. Kyle and Elijah haven't been starting a band yet. They need to find a lead singer. ☐
   _____
3. How long have you been learning Chinese, Kim? ☐
   _____
4. Rachel and Destiny have created a vlog about DIY and hackerspaces for girls. ☐
   _____
5. Mackenzie has been attending acting classes at the community center for some months now. ☐
   _____

6 Mark (✓) the correct sentence for each picture.

1.
☐ Kaylee has finished packing. She's ready to travel abroad.
☐ Kaylee has been packing for hours. She's not ready to travel abroad.

2.
☐ My father has written a book about DIY. He's in an autograph session now.
☐ My father has been writing a book about DIY for 2 years. He's in a meeting with his editor now.

3.
☐ Anna has flown her drone over the city. She's fixing it now.
☐ Anna has been flying her drone over the city since early this morning.

1 **Complete the sentences according to the pictures. Then use the letters above the numbers to complete the last sentence.**

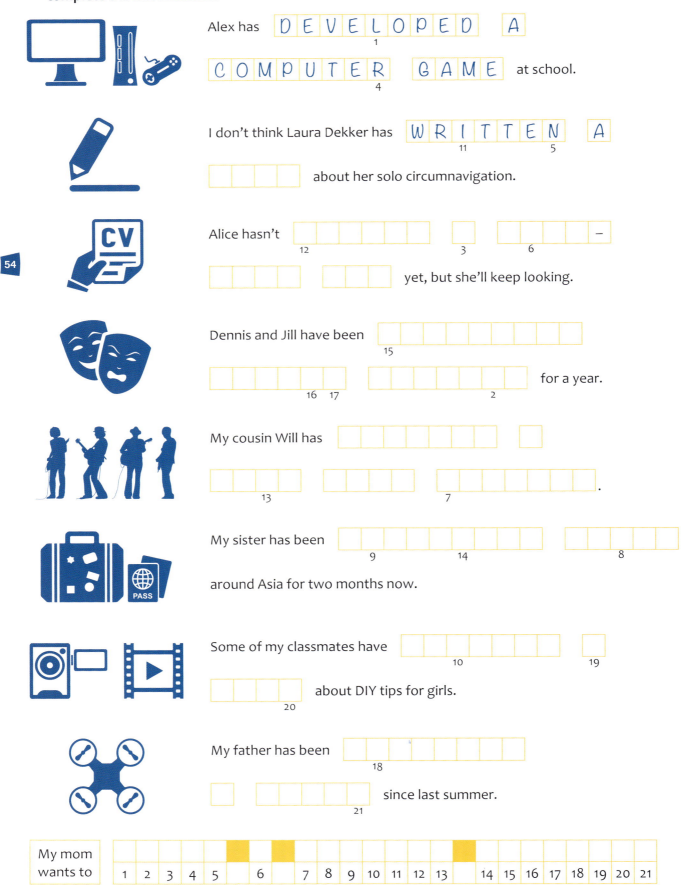

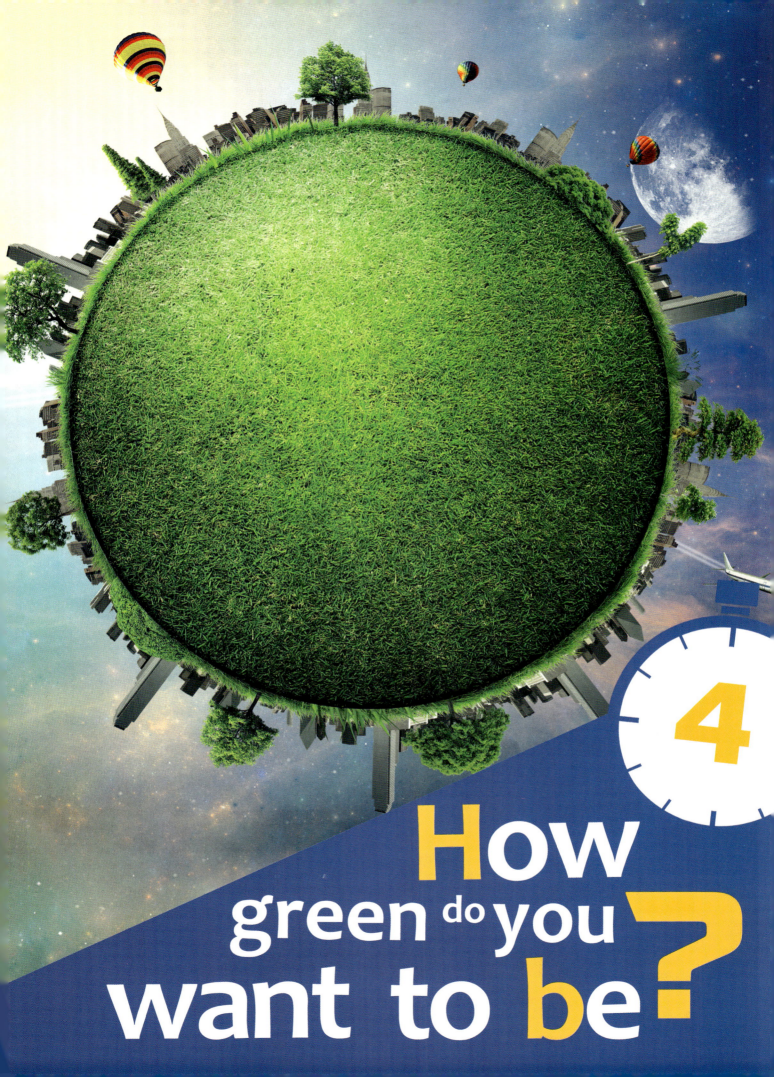

JUST GO GREEN!

There are simple attitudes we can adopt in our everyday lives to contribute to a sustainable planet!

Go green when you're cleaning!

You can eliminate products full of chemicals and replace them with natural products. _____, for example, has more use than only adding taste to your salad – it is great to clean carpets and windows! And _____ is great for doing the laundry.

Go green when you're eating!

Have you ever considered growing your own vegetables? Even if there isn't a yard in your house, you can use tiny spaces such as your window to have an _____. Besides helping the environment, producing (part of) the food on your plate will give you a sense of achievement.

Another great help is to keep and eat _____. Food waste has a huge impact on the environment—tons of resources, such as water and electricity, are wasted with the tons of food that go to the garbage every day.

Go green when you're getting around!

The _____ is a fantastic option for short distances, like going to school or **running errands**. It's cheap, green and you'll look cool to your friends! When going to further places with friends, consider organizing a _____ with your friends' parents, instead of asking your mom or dad to take you. You'll be helping the environment (and your parents will be happy sharing the task with other people).

56

Vocabulary

1 Look at the pictures. What do you know about the products or actions shown below?

baking soda

rechargeable batteries

car pool

reusable shopping bags

food leftovers

electric bike

white vinegar

indoor garden

2 Read and complete the texts with the words in Activity 1.

_____ are already popular and even fashionable. There are some models that can be folded and easily kept in your backpack. There's no excuse to use plastic shopping bags anymore. Electronics can also be green. Estimates show that every family throws away eight batteries per year. Using _____ simply eliminates this disposal.

3 🎧¹⁵ Listen to people talking about the green actions in the texts. Mark (✓) the actions they mention.

	Carry a	Clean clothes with	Grow an	Ride an	Use	Organize a
1. Hailey and Sydney						
2. Tyler and Abbie						
3. Anna and Brian						
4. Megan and Ben						

4 Rank the green attitudes in this section.

The Greenest

⟵⟶

The Least Green

5 Work with a partner. Answer the questions below.

1. Do you have a reusable shopping bag? How often do you use it?
2. Have you ever tried to use vinegar or baking soda to clean things around your house?
3. Would you like to have an electric bike? Why (not)?
4. What are the advantages of organizing a car pool? Can you think of any disadvantages?

Guess What!
Years these products take to decompose in nature:
batteries – up to 100 years
plastic bags – 10–20 years
napkins – 2–4 weeks

Glossary
run errands: a short and quick journey to do something

57

Grammar

1 Read about actions that help save the environment. Mark (✓) the one that depends on an individual attitude.

The Enviroment What If...?

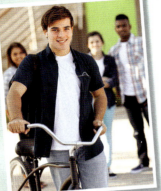

It's our responsibility to take care of our environment. We can imagine some possible actions we can take ourselves or consider hypothetical situations in order to act for change. Look at two ideas:

How much gas will I save if I ride my bike to school every day? ☐
A lot! If you live 2 km away and ride your bike to school every day, you will save over 167 liters of gas in one year! Also, you will save 395 kg of CO2 emissions. In terms of health benefits, you will certainly become fit if you ride 4 km per day. And your mom and dad will be happy—if you get to school by yourself, they won't have to worry about who will take and pick you up anymore.

What would happen if people simply stopped using plastic bags? ☐
Eliminating plastic bags completely is almost impossible. But if people stopped using plastic bags when shopping, plastic trash would drop dramatically—just one supermarket chain in the United States wouldn't need to buy 1.8 billion bags every year anymore! Besides the benefit of having less garbage in landfills, if we replaced shopping plastic bags with reusable bags, tons of resources would be saved as well.

2 Read the article again. Then circle the correct answer.

1. This action refers to a hypothetical situation, which is not likely to happen: Action 1   Action 2
2. This action refers to a possible situation, which might happen: Action 1   Action 2

First Conditional – Real, Possible Situations

Condition	Result
If you ride your bike to school every day,	you will save over 167 liters of gas in one year.
If + subject + verb	*subject + will + verb*

Second Conditional – Unreal Situations

Condition	Result
If people stopped using plastic bags,	plastic trash would drop dramatically.
If + subject + verb	*subject + would + verb*

3 Use the code below to identify the structures in Activity 1.

Circle	Condition clauses in the First Conditional
Highlight in yellow	Result clauses in the First Conditional
Underline	Condition clauses in the Second Conditional
Highlight in green	Result clauses in the Second Conditional

4 **Match the sentence halves.**

If my dad gives me an electric bike for Christmas,…

Would you use vinegar and baking soda…

If Eric's mom didn't organize the car pool,…

My family and the neighbors will start a community garden…

Will you eat the leftovers from yesterday's dinner…

Danny wouldn't recycle the shopping bags…

if you had to clean the whole house?

if we get permission from the City Council to use an abandoned area near my house.

if I make a nice salad to go with them?

I will use it to go to school every day.

if we didn't convince him to do it.

I would have to walk to school three times a week.

5 **Complete the conversations. Use the first or second conditionals.**

1. Kylie: What are you doing standing here at the park, Jake?
   Jake: I'm recharging my electric bike. If I _____ (do – neg), I _____ (ride – neg) it to school tomorrow.

2. Hailey: Look at all this trash… it's so sad!
   Ethan: It sure is. If plastic bags _____ (be) banned, they _____ (end up – neg) on the beach.

3. Chris: _____ you _____ (help) us create the community garden if the City Council _____ (give) us permission to do so?
   Tony: Of course I will!

4. Jasmine: Imagine this situation. You found out your favorite brand of chocolate polluted the environment. _____ you _____ (continue) to buy their products?
   Tyler: No, I wouldn't. I think pollution is a serious environmental problem.

6 **Now number the pictures according to the conversations in Activity 5 they refer to.**

7 **Think Fast! Complete the sentences using your own ideas.**

1. If I could do only one thing to help save the environment, I would _____.
2. I will / won't ride a bike to school if _____.

Listening and Writing

1 Read the biodata of Ellen Parker, who was interviewed for a podcast. What do you think she will talk about?

Dr. Ellen Parker has a Ph.D. in Climate Variability and Impacts from the Massachusetts Institute of Technology (MIT), and is one of the world's most famous specialists on climate change. She has worked as a professor at several universities around the world and is also a consultant with the United Nations Environment Program (UNEP).

2 🎧¹⁶ Now listen to the interview. Check your predictions in Activity 1.

3 🎧¹⁶ Listen to the interview again. Complete the summary with the words from the box.

> 17   destructive   hurricanes   islands   stronger   NASA
> 1880   1970   20th   The American Meteorologist Society

Be Strategic!
When listening, it is important to be able to notice the difference between opinions (people's feelings), facts (statements that can be proven right or wrong) and supporting **evidence** for the facts.

Effect #1: The sea level is rising.

Who is saying that?   1. _____ satellites.
How much did it rise?   2. _____ centimeters.
When did it happen?   In the 3. _____ century.
Consequence?   If sea levels continue to rise, some
                             4. _____ will disappear.

Effect #2: The planet is getting warmer.

When did the temperature start rising?   In 5. _____.
When did the warming become more intense?   In 6. _____.
Who registered the warmest years?   7. _____
Consequence?   If the average temperature increases
                                              by 2° C, 8. _____ will get
                                              9. _____ and more
                                              10. _____.

4 🎧¹⁶ Listen to the interview once more. Label the items in the interview according to the code below.
- Opinion (O)   - Fact (F)   - Supporting evidence for the fact (SE)

1. "I think these people are afraid of facing climate change." ☐
2. "The level of the sea is rising." ☐
3. "According to NASA satellites, it rose 17 centimeters in the 20th century." ☐
4. "That sounds terrible!" ☐
5. "The planet is getting warmer." ☐
6. "Meteorologic registers show that the global temperature has been rising since 1880." ☐
7. "… according to the American Meteorologist Society, the ten warmest years have all happened between 1998 and 2014!" ☐
8. "I believe that governments must take action to stop global warming, and they must do it now!" ☐

The Gazette

The School Newspaper — thegazette.com — Monday — December 2

5 Now read this report about a green initiative in a high school. Then answer the questions below in your notebook.

Green Initiative: Greenville High School Community Garden
Year Report

Last year, we decided to start a community garden in our school. After a home economics class on organic produce, we thought it would be a good idea to use an abandoned area of **soil** in the schoolyard to grow healthy vegetables and herbs to be used in the school kitchen.

- **Money:** The school gave the group $230 to spend on seeds and gardening tools.
- **Training:** A certified gardener gave students a course on organic gardening.

KALE

The results are:
- Five different vegetables and herbs (tomatoes, kale, lettuce, parsley and chives) are being grown.
- Around 124 students are involved.
- After six months, 10% of the vegetables used in the school lunch for students were replaced with organic products from our garden.
- The remaining products that are not used in the school kitchen, such as the herbs, are distributed to school neighbors once a week.

1. What was the initiative?
2. Why did the students decide to do it?
3. What did they need to develop the initiative?
4. What were two results of the initiative?

6 Think Fast! Can you label four of the vegetables and herbs below in your language and in English? They are all mentioned in the report!

7 Now you are going to research and write a report on a green initiative in your country or around the world. Use the chart to outline your report in your notebook.

What was the initiative?	Where and why did people decide to develop it?	What did people need to develop it?	What were the results?

Glossary

evidence: information that proves that something is true or exists

soil: firm land not covered with concrete

8 Now write your report in your notebook. Then present it to the class.

Culture

1 What do you know about Sweden? Circle the options in the chart. The pictures in the brochure will help you.

Capital	Climate	Two Tourist Attractions	Other Important Facts
Lapland	Tropical	Gamla Stan and Drottningholm Palace	It is the largest Scandinavian country.
Malmo	Temperate/Subarctic	Malmo and Stockholm	Its healthcare system is one of the best in the world.
Stockholm	Mediterranean	Lapland and Uppsala	Environmental issues are important.

River in Lapland, north of Sweden, in the Winter

Visit Sweden!

View of the historic Old Town (Gamla Stan) in Stockholm

Drottningholm Palace, the private residence of the Swedish Royal Family, visited by millions of people every year

Guess What!
Sweden is the third largest country in Europe, but it has the second lowest population density, with only 23.5 people living per square km (km2).

2 Read the text about some green initiatives in Sweden. Then write YES or NO for the statements below.

SWEDEN – THE GREENEST COUNTRY IN THE WORLD

Located in Northern Europe, Sweden is famous for its high quality of life and its cold weather. It is also famous for using energy from renewable sources. Recently, the Scandinavian country has become famous for a series of green initiatives that aim to create a sustainable country. Here are three of them:

Green Roofs
Augustenborg, in the suburbs of Malmo—the third largest city in Sweden—is considered the greenest neighborhood in the world. On the top of private and public buildings in the area, the city government has planted over 10,000 colorful and beautiful gardens, which can be visited. The green roofs, among other things, provide a better climate and contribute to urban biodiversity. Malmo's government also invests in solar panels for energy and in waste recycling.

Urban Farming
Community and indoor gardens have been popular all over Sweden for a long time and enjoyed as a hobby by many. Now, more than a pastime, people see it as a way of life—of a healthier life—and also as a manner of saying "no" to excessive consumerism. One Swedish gardening enthusiast says, "Gardening is basically a fun way of changing our habits, instead of just getting depressed about the state of the world. You get happy growing, green makes you happy."

Vintage Clothing
Swedes are big fans of buying second hand clothes! They are sold at regular stores and also at specific clothing fairs, such as Vintagemassan, in Stockholm.

Besides the vintage market, Swedish fashion companies have their own green initiatives. Fashion brand Filippa K sells sustainable jeans, produced with minimal impact on the environment. Also, customers can rent clothes at the brand's stores—paying 20% of the full price—and return them after four days.

1. Sweden is considered the most ecological country on our planet.
2. The inhabitants from Augustenborg are responsible for planting the roof gardens.
3. The green roofs are the only ecological initiatives developed by the city government in Malmo.
4. Urban farming is a recent trend among people in Sweden.
5. Swedes see urban farming as a way of reducing purchases at supermarkets.
6. A brand in Sweden allows people to pay to wear clothes for a few days and return them to the store.

3 🎧17 Listen to two conversations. Mark (✓) the green initiative they are talking about.

	Green Roofs	Urban Farming	Vintage Clothing
Conversation 1			
Conversation 2			

 Stop and Think! Which of the initiatives in Activity 2 could be taken in your city or country? Why?

Project

1 How green is your school? Look at the quiz about eco-friendly attitudes and mark (✓) the ones your school already adopts. Then read the results.

QUIZ — HOW GREEN IS YOUR SCHOOL?

Initiative

1. There are specific bins for recyclable items in my school. ☐
2. The recyclable trash in the bins is sent to recycling facilities. ☐
3. There is a community garden in my school. ☐
4. There are organic food options in the school cafeteria. ☐
5. We discuss the protection of the environment and sustainability in our classes. ☐
6. School staff uses certified green cleaners, or natural cleaners such as white vinegar. ☐
7. There is a "turn it off" policy at school (i.e., students and staff know they should turn off lights in empty rooms, turn off computers, printers, etc.). ☐
8. Daylight is used efficiently (e.g., there are big windows in the classroom, so that we don't need to turn on the lights during the day). ☐
9. Most of the equipment in our school is energy efficient. ☐
10. Students and staff are encouraged to walk or ride a bike to school. ☐
11. There is a specific place for students and staff to safely park their bikes. ☐
12. In the restrooms, there are automatic faucets to save water. ☐
13. Reused school material is popular among students. ☐
14. The use of rechargeable batteries is promoted. ☐

Results:

12-14 points: Your school rocks! Students and staff are champions for the green cause!

8-10 points: You're all doing a great job and you're ready to take further steps to become even greener.

5-7 points: Your school has started the green journey. Keep working hard!

0-4 points: It seems your school has just started to adopt a green attitude. There's potential, but you should all work together to get greener—and soon!

2 Work in small groups. Based on the result above, choose a green initiative you would like to implement in your school. You can even use one of the actions in the quiz.

3 Now brainstorm ideas for an action plan to implement your initiative. Look at the example below.

Action Plan
Goal: Create a Community Garden in Our School
Team Members: Kylie, Mike, Danny, Martina, Ben and Leah

Task	Key Activities	Point Person	Begin Date	End Date	Status
1. Get permission to use an area in the schoolyard to create the garden.	– Collect information about the advantages of a community garden. – Talk to our principal to get permission.	– Kylie – Whole team	Mar 14 Mar 21 (set meeting w/ Mrs. Jones)	Mar 20 Mar 21	
2. Learn how to design a garden.	– Talk to Mr. Spencer (Kylie's grandpa) about the best vegetables for our garden. – Read about the best practices for community gardens. – Share knowledge with all the members of the team.	– Kylie and Mike – Danny and Martina – Whole team	Mar 22 Mar 22 Mar 25	Mar 22 Mar 24 Mar 25	

4 Write your own plan on a separate sheet of paper. Follow the steps below.

Step 1: Divide your goal into tasks, and then consider the key activities for each task.

Step 2: Discuss, in your group, the activities each of you will be responsible for.

Step 3: Set begin and end dates for each activity.
Tip! Try to be as realistic as possible with your dates.

5 Now present your action plan to the class.

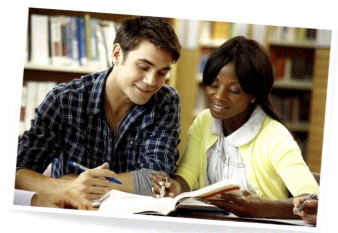

Stop and Think! Which action plan would have more of a chance to be implemented in your school? Why?

Review

1 **Complete the crossword puzzle. Use the sentence hints to help you.**

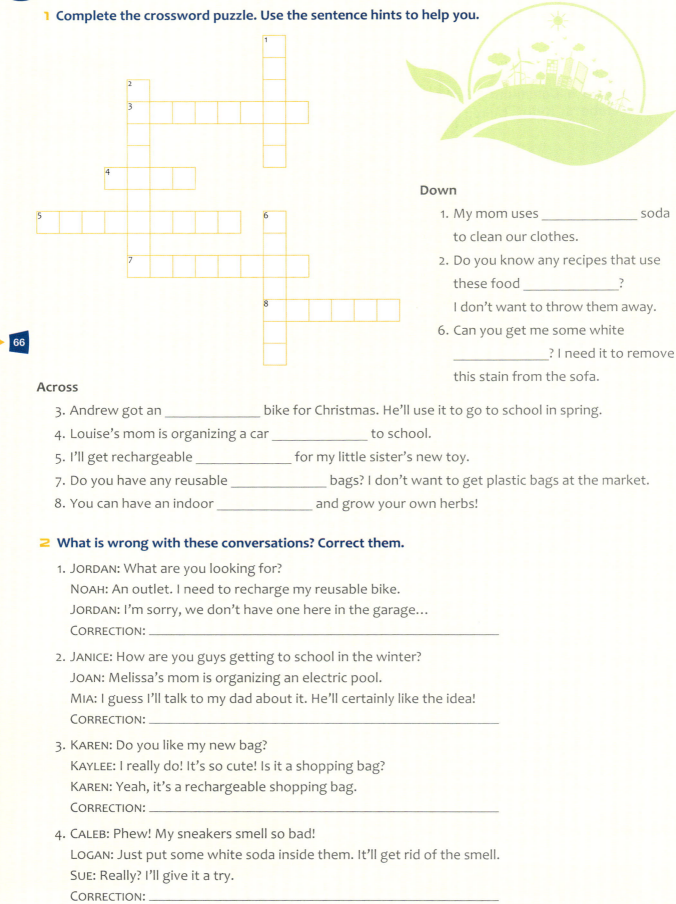

Down

1. My mom uses _____ soda to clean our clothes.
2. Do you know any recipes that use these food _____? I don't want to throw them away.
6. Can you get me some white _____? I need it to remove this stain from the sofa.

Across

3. Andrew got an _____ bike for Christmas. He'll use it to go to school in spring.
4. Louise's mom is organizing a car _____ to school.
5. I'll get rechargeable _____ for my little sister's new toy.
7. Do you have any reusable _____ bags? I don't want to get plastic bags at the market.
8. You can have an indoor _____ and grow your own herbs!

2 **What is wrong with these conversations? Correct them.**

1. JORDAN: What are you looking for?
   NOAH: An outlet. I need to recharge my reusable bike.
   JORDAN: I'm sorry, we don't have one here in the garage…
   CORRECTION: _____

2. JANICE: How are you guys getting to school in the winter?
   JOAN: Melissa's mom is organizing an electric pool.
   MIA: I guess I'll talk to my dad about it. He'll certainly like the idea!
   CORRECTION: _____

3. KAREN: Do you like my new bag?
   KAYLEE: I really do! It's so cute! Is it a shopping bag?
   KAREN: Yeah, it's a rechargeable shopping bag.
   CORRECTION: _____

4. CALEB: Phew! My sneakers smell so bad!
   LOGAN: Just put some white soda inside them. It'll get rid of the smell.
   SUE: Really? I'll give it a try.
   CORRECTION: _____

3 **Complete the short conversations. Use the first conditional.**

1. ERIC: What _____ you _____ (do) if the principal _____ (remove) the recycling bins from school?
   JULIA: I _____ probably _____ (put) any recyclable items in my bag and _____ (take) them to a recycling facility near my house.

2. NICOLE: If I _____ (plug) my electric bike in to this outlet, how long _____ it _____ (take) to recharge it?
   CHLOE: Hmm… I'm not sure. Why don't you check its user manual?

3. ROB: If we _____ (move) to the countryside, my dad said he _____ (build) a passive house for us.
   MORGAN: Really? I _____ definitely _____ (visit) you if your dad _____ (do) that!

4. RACHEL: According to this article, if we _____ (start – neg) doing something about global warming now, we _____ (be able to – neg) to stop climate change.
   MEGAN: This is a very serious thing. We _____ _____ (have) a planet for our children if things _____ (continue) as they are…

4 **Write sentences from the prompts in your notebook. Use the second conditional.**

1. I / become a millionaire → I / donate some money to protect the rainforest

2. we / stop drinking bottled water → tons of plastic / be saved

3. Americans / replace one regular light bulb with a fluorescent bulb → the pollution reduction / be the same as removing one million cars from the streets

4. people / not pre-heat their ovens when cooking → they / pay less on their gas or electricity bills

5. my mom / be allowed to work from home → she / spend less time in traffic and save gas

5 **Rewrite the sentences below. Use the first or the second conditional.**

1. We'd love to grow a community garden in our school, but we don't have an area with soil in the schoolyard.
   _____

2. I hope I have time to attend the gardening workshop on the weekend.
   _____

3. My mom would like to organize a car pool to work, but her co-workers live far from our house.
   _____

4. I want to make a sandwich with some chicken leftovers when I get home, but my sister wants to make a soup with them.
   _____

67

Just for Fun

1 Use the words in the cloud to complete eight attitudes that help the environment.

rechargeable indoor pool garden car
electric bag shopping white food
soda vinegar reusable
bike baking leftovers batteries

1. Organize a _____ _____ to get to school, so that more people travel in one car.
2. Carry a _____ _____ _____ inside your regular bag, so that you don't need to use plastic bags when going to the supermarket.
3. Consider buying an _____ _____—it's an eco-friendly and cool way to get around.
4. Try using _____ _____ and _____ _____ when cleaning your house.
5. Grow some vegetables and herbs in an _____ _____—they are healthier than goods found at the grocery store.
6. Start using _____ _____ in electronic equipment in your house—they are cheaper and greener than the traditional ones.
7. Don't throw away _____ _____—they can be "recycled" into new (and delicious) dishes or snacks.

2 Complete these lyrics with the verbs in the box. Use the first or second conditional.

ask   be (2x)   dance   fall   find   have   look   lose   save   see   stand up   think   walk

If you're lost, you can look and you 1. _____ me
Time after time
If you 2. _____ I will catch you, I'll be waiting
Time after time
("Time After Time" – Cindy Lauper)

What 3. _____ you _____ if I sang out of tune
4. _____ you _____ and walk out on me?
("With A Little Help From My Friends" – The Beatles)

'Cause there'll be no sunlight
If I 5. _____ you, baby
There 6. _____ no clear skies
If I lose you, baby
Just like the clouds
My eyes will do the same, if you
7. _____ away
Everyday it'll rain
("It Will Rain" – Bruno Mars)

_____ you 8. _____ if I asked you to dance?
_____ you run and never 9. _____ back?
Would you cry if you 10. _____ me crying?
_____ you 11. _____ my soul tonight?
("Hero" – Enrique Iglesias)

If God 12. _____ a name, what would it be?
And would you call it to his face,
If you 13. _____ faced with Him in all His glory?
What 14. _____ you _____ if you had just one question?
("One of Us" – Joan Osborne)

1 Five pictures are missing from the article. Read it and then number the images on the right as they should be placed in the text.

Eight Things, Creatures and Phenomena Some People Believe in, but Scientists Don't!

1 Can people actually communicate with each other's minds, without using words? Although there has been no scientific evidence, lots of people do believe in **telepathy**.

2 These creatures have their origins in oral stories told in countries in West Africa. Nowadays, we can see **zombies** depicted in horror literature and TV series— but that's all.

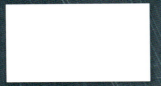

3 Is there intelligent life on other planets? If so, are these creatures among us? Independent scientists and even governments have invested time and money to find evidence of **aliens**.

4 Speaking of aliens, how do they come to "visit" Earth? Sightings of alien "spaceships," also called unidentified flying objects, or **UFOs**, have been registered throughout history.

5 The apparition of a dead person's spirit is called by different names—specter, soul and phantom, among others. Many people claim to have seen **ghosts**, and this belief is present in cultures on all continents.

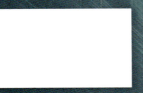

6 Man, wolf... or both? This is another creature whose mythology has been present in a wide range of cultures, since ancient Greece. **Werewolves** have also become popular due to literature and pop culture.

7 Are there people who can see things, people and events that are distant, both in space and time? Claims for **clairvoyance** have been supported by personal accounts, but not by scientific evidence.

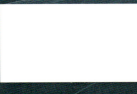

8 Is it possible for someone to move or even change the shape of an object without touching it? Many people believe in the power of **telekinesis**, but all experiments to prove it have been criticized by science.

2 Organize the phenomena, things and creatures in Activity 1 in the chart below.

Extrasensory Perception (ESP)	Extraterrestrial	Supernatural Creatures

Guess What!
The most famous alleged UFO incident in history happened in Roswell, New Mexico (USA), in 1947. The US Air Force claimed that the aircraft that crashed at a ranch was a surveillance balloon, but since then several conspiracy theories have been elaborated—all of them involving aliens!

3 🎧¹⁸ Listen to a scientist providing explanations for three of the items in Activity 1. Number the creatures and phenomena she talks about.

- Clairvoyance ☐
- Ghosts ☐
- Telekinesis ☐
- Telepathy ☐
- UFO Sightings ☐
- Zombies ☐

4 Answer the questions below.

1. Have you ever seen something unexplainable? If so, how did you feel?
   _____.

2. In your opinion, why are creatures such as zombies so popular nowadays?
   _____.

3. Do you believe people can foresee events in the future?
   _____.

4. Do you think there is intelligent life on other planets?
   _____.

5 Share your ideas in Activity 4 with a partner.

Stop and Think! Why are people so interested in supernatural phenomena?

Grammar

UNSOLVED MYSTERIES

1 Read the unsolved mysteries. Then mark (✓) in the chart below which story each possible explanation refers to.

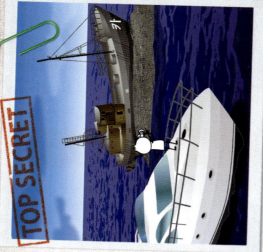

TOP SECRET

Story #2: Ghost Ships on the Coast of Japan

Over the years, several boats have been found **drifting** off the coast of Japan. Most of them were empty, while others held bodily remains and skeletons.

The boats were in terrible condition and badly equipped for fishing—they didn't have GPS devices or even a radio. The type of equipment and signs written on them indicate they all came from North Korea.

Since there are no official diplomatic channels between Tokyo and Pyongyang, nobody really knows why the boats ended up on the Japanese coast, why some of them were empty or how the fishermen died.

🔍 Guess What!

North Korea, whose capital is Pyongyang, is the most mysterious country in the world. Located in East Asia, few foreigners are allowed to visit it and its residents can't leave the country.

Modals of Speculation – Past: *Must have, Might have and Could have*

```
+  Totally possible                              Absolutely possible
      must have ─── might have ─── could have
   ─────────────────────────────────────────→
      couldn't have ─ must not have ─ might not have
-
```

must	
might **have** built the statues on the island.	
could	

Aliens

modal + *have* + past participle

TOP SECRET

Story #1: Blobs Falling from the Sky

In August, 1994, people living in Oakland, Washington, USA, woke up to the sound of rain. However, they noticed that the substance falling from the sky was not the usual drops of water, but a gelatinous, clear substance, similar to **jellyfish**.

An initial analysis of the blobs showed that they contained human **white blood cells** and two types of bacteria, but it couldn't confirm their origin.

Several residents got sick, and pets who were in contact with the substance died. People claim they saw Air Force planes slowly flying over the city for several days prior to the incident.

Possible Explanation

	Story #1	Story #2
1. Aliens abducted the men, who could have been used in experiments in spaceships.		
2. Since the US military was testing bombs in the Pacific, the abnormal substance must have been the result of the destruction of a school of sea animals.		
3. Aliens might have been eliminating human cells and bacteria from their spaceships, after carrying out several experiments.		
4. The men were sent to sea by their government in order to fish and bring food back to the country. However, their ships were old and not equipped for the journey, and they were not able to return home.		

72

2 Complete the sentences with the past form of the modals and the verbs in parentheses.

Built around 3000 B.C., Stonehenge, located in England, is one of the most mysterious monuments in the world. But who
1. _____ it? (could – build)
According to studies, different ancient civilizations _____ it, over a few centuries. And there are several fair theories that try to explain why it was built.
2. _____ (might – do)
One of them suggests that Stonehenge 3. _____ (might – be) for ordinary people, a cemetery, but it 4. _____ (might not – be) since the artifacts found there indicate that rich or religious people
5. _____ in the graves. (must – be buried)

3 Use the prompts to speculate about the stories in Activity 1. Use must (not) have, could / couldn't have, and might (not) have, according to how certain you think each explanation is.

1. Aliens / abduct / the men on the ship
   _____.
2. The blobs / be / pieces of jellyfish from an explosion
   _____.
3. Aliens / discard / their experiments over Oakland
   _____.
4. North Korea / send / fishermen to sea with poor equipment
   _____.

4 🎧 19 Listen to a radio report about a strange phenomenon. Then write sentences in your notebook with possible explanations, according to different people.

Mrs. Strickland
- She saw lights in the sky.
- Her cat, Fluffy, disappeared.

The Military Staff
- They tested meteorological balloons.
- The chance of the lights being a sign of alien activity.

Astronomers

- They noticed unusual meteor activity in the area.

 Stop and Think! What is the best explanation for the unsolved mysteries in Activity 4? Why?

5 Think Fast! Work with a partner. Can you come up with another explanation for the lights in Springville?

Glossary
blob: a small amount of thick liquid
jellyfish: a round, soft and translucent sea animal
white blood cells: cells that protect our body from illnesses
drift: move slowly on water

Reading and Writing

1 Read these reports of famous disappearances. Underline the most appropriate title for each document.

The Death of the Grand Dame of Mystery

Famous Aviator Rescued from the Sea

Agatha Christie and her daughter Rosalind are featured in a newspaper article about the writer's mysterious disappearance.

Who? Agatha Christie, one of the most popular writers of the 20th century
Where? From her house, in southeast England
When? In 1926

Born in England on September 15, 1890, Agatha Christie sold billions of novels, making her the most famous mystery writer in the world.

An episode of the writer's life, however, seems more like one of her stories than reality. On a cold night in December, 1926, she left her house in her car, leaving a strange note claiming she would go on vacation.

Christie's family notified the police, who started to search for her. The car was found abandoned on the **edge** of a **quarry**, not far from the house. The **hood** was up and the lights were on, but there was no sign of Christie.

One of the largest searches for a person in history began. Thousands of police officers and volunteers looked for Christie, with no success.

The writer was finally recognized by a musician in a hotel over 350 km away from her house. She had remained missing for 11 days. Christie never clearly explained her disappearance

Status: UNSOLVED

Amelia Earhart sitting in the cockpit of her Lockheed Electra—the same airplane in which she vanished in 1937.

Who? Amelia Earhart, the first woman to fly across the Atlantic Ocean by herself
Where? Somewhere in the Pacific Ocean
When? In 1937

Born on July 24, 1897, Earhart was an American aviator, a magazine editor, the vice president of an airline company and an activist for the advancement of female pilots.

Nine years after flying across the Atlantic, Earhart took on a new challenge. On June 1, 1937, the female aviator and another pilot, Fred Noonan, took off from Florida to fly around the world on a route over the equator.

The journey, however, was difficult—Earhart and Noonan faced problems during different **legs** of the trip. On July 2, 1937, Earhart and Noonan took off for another (and final) leg of the journey: they were supposed to fly from New Guinea to Howland Island, a **tiny** strip of land in the middle of the Pacific. But they never make it to their destination.

The US government undertook search missions in the surroundings of Howland Island for several weeks, but Earhart's plane has never been found.

Status: UNSOLVED

The Mysterious Disappearance of an American Legend

THE MOST MYSTERIOUS DAYS OF A MYSTERY WRITER

2 Compare and contrast Amelia Earhart's and Agatha Christie's stories. Organize your ideas in the diagram, writing at least three things for each item.

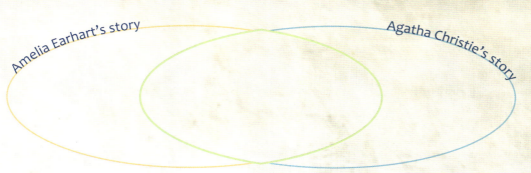

Be Strategic! Graphic organizers can help us organize the main information in a text. Venn diagrams are useful to categorize information according to similarities and differences between texts.

3 Now read some theories for the disappearances of Amelia Earhart and Agatha Christie. Which do you think is the best? Discuss with your classmates and teacher.

Why did Amelia Earhart disappear?

Most people believe that Earhart and Noonan must have gotten lost due to navigation mistakes and couldn't find Howland Island. They must have run out of fuel and had to **ditch** in the sea.

Another theory claims that the pilots might have landed on another island in the Pacific, where they might have been able to live for some time. A less credible theory suggests that Earhart and Noonan could have been on a spy mission and could have been captured by the Japanese.

Why did Agatha Christie disappear?

Public opinion offered different explanations for the famous novelist's disappearance. Some people say that she might have had a serious argument with her husband and then decided to leave their house. Others believe that her disappearance could have been a publicity stunt for her latest novel.

A more recent theory strongly suggests that Christie must have suffered from "out-of-body amnesia" or "fugue state," a medical condition in which the affected person gets confused about his/her identity and usually runs away from home.

4 In your notebook, write another explanation for Earhart's and Christie's disappearances. Follow the steps below.

Step 1: Read the stories on p. 74 again. Also, read the explanations in Activity 3.

Step 2: Write your explanation. Think about which modal verbs you can use, considering how credible your theory is.

Step 3: When you have finished, share your theory with a classmate. Get feedback from him / her about language use and the consistency of your story.

 **Stop and Think!** Work in small groups. Read your theories out loud. Which is the most credible? Why?

Glossary
leg: part of a long trip
tiny: very small
edge: the end of an area
quarry: an excavation from which workers get stones
hood: the metal cover of the engine of a car
to ditch: to crash-land in the sea

Culture

1 What do you know about the Nazca Lines? Discuss with a classmate. The captions of the pictures will help you.

The Nazca Desert, in southern Peru

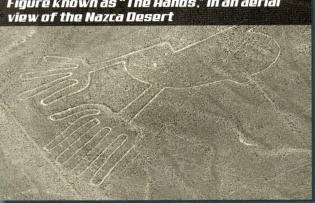
Figure known as "The Hands," in an aerial view of the Nazca Desert

Hummingbird figure in an aerial view of the Nazca Desert

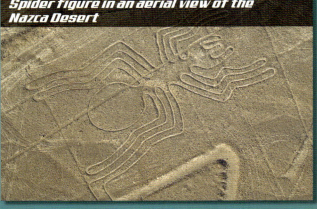
Spider figure in an aerial view of the Nazca Desert

Location of the Nazca Lines, in the Nazca Desert, in Peru

Illustration of a set of figures depicted in the Nazca Desert

2 Think Fast! Mention a strange or mysterious event or place in your country which scientists can't totally explain.

3 Read an encyclopedia article about the Nazca Lines. Then complete the fact file.

Article   Talk   Read   Edit   View history   Search

Nazca Lines

Located in the Nazca Desert, in southern Peru, the Nazca Lines are a set of large designs created on the **ground** (called geoglyphs) by the Nazca people, over 2,000 years ago. They can be seen from the air, or from the top of the mountains in the desert, and are spread over an area of 500 km².

Most of the designs depict animals and plants, such as a whale (65 meters long), a spider (46 meters long), and a hummingbird (50 meters long). They were discovered in the 1920s, when commercial air travel became popular in Peru, and although archaeologists and other scientists have offered several explanations about why and how the figures were made, none of them has been widely accepted.

Fortunately, the dry weather and winds have helped to preserve the geoglyphs naturally over the centuries. Nowadays, the Nazca Lines are considered a World Heritage Site by UNESCO, and thousands of tourists fly over them to wonder about their mystery every year.

Click here to continue reading   77

Guess What!
World Heritage Sites are places that have a special cultural or natural interest, according to the United Nations Educational, Scientific and Cultural Organization (UNESCO). There are almost 1,000 sites listed around the world.

Fact File – Nazca Lines
Location:
Date of construction:
Area:
Types of geoglyphs:
Date of discovery:
Listed by UNESCO as:

4 🎧 20 Listen to two people talking about some possible explanations for the Nazca Lines. Complete the explanations with the words from the box.

> aliens   gods   map   planets   processions   roads   sky

THEORY 1: The Nazca lines could have been Incan _____.

THEORY 2: They must have been paths for religious _____.

THEORY 3: The Nazca people might have made the drawings in order to be seen by their _____ from the _____.

THEORY 4: The Nazca lines could have been an astronomic _____, indicating the position of _____ and stars.

THEORY 5: _____ could have created the lines, not the Nazca people.

Glossary
hummingbird: a very small bird whose wings move very fast
ground: the surface of the earth
the Incas: a people who lived in Peru and had an empire in the area before the Spanish conquest
path: a track for people to walk on

 Stop and Think! What is the best theory for the Nazca Lines? Why?

Project

1 Look at the slides of a presentation about a famous unsolved mystery. Number the slides in the order you think they were presented.

I WANT YOU TO SIT NEXT TO ME. YOU ARE BEING HIJACKED.

When the plane landed in Reno...

When the plane landed in Seattle...
- an airline agent gave him the money.
- the plane was refueled.
- Cooper released the passengers and part of the crew.

When the plane took off from Seattle...
- Destination: Reno, Nevada

His demands:
- US $200,000.00
- 4 parachutes
- a fuel truck to refuel the plane in Seattle

Who was D.B. Cooper?
- Unidentified man
- Hijacked a Boeing 727 on Nov. 24, 1971
- Plane route:

Unsolved Mysteries

D. B. Cooper

Glossary

digital recorder

2 🎧²¹ Now listen to the presentation. Check the order of the slides in Activity 1.

3 Work in small groups. Make a presentation about an unsolved mystery. Follow the steps below.

Step 1:

Research an unsolved mystery—either in your country or abroad. Collect as much information as possible about it, such as:
- pictures
- official information
- media reports
- witnesses' accounts

If they exist, gather different theories that explain what happened.

Step 2:

Organize your information into slides, using a slide show presentation program, if available.

- Use attractive layouts and clear fonts for the text.
- Add pictures, photos or other visual elements related to your mystery.
- Don't write on the slides all the text of the story you are going to tell—include only key words and information, using bullet points.

Step 3:

Once your slides are ready, rehearse your presentation!

- Decide who is going to be in charge of each section.
- You can use a cell phone or a **digital recorder** to record your rehearsal, so that you can listen and improve your performance.

4 Ready? Make your presentation to the other groups.

 Stop and Think! Which presentation did you like best? Why?

Review

1 Complete the sentences. Then number the pictures according to the description they refer to.

1. _____ appeared in an American movie for the first time in 1932. They were presented as creatures who were "undead."

2. From E.T. to Superman, _____ have been depicted in many famous Hollywood movies, but there's no scientific evidence we have received visitors from other planets.

3. _____ are also seen in movies, but usually not as protagonists. Jacob in the *Twilight* series and Remus Lupin in the *Harry Potter* series are famous examples of these anthropomorphic creatures in the movies.

4. There are lots of horror movies about _____. *The Grudge* is one of the most famous movies about souls that have come back from the world of the dead.

2 Complete the definitions with the correct word.

Telepathy

_____ is the so-called ability to move an object without making any physical contact with it.

Telekinesis

_____ is the supposed ability to predict future events and/or see people and events that are far away.

Clairvoyance

_____ is the apparent ability to communicate thoughts from one's mind to another person's mind.

3 Decide if the sentences are right (R) or wrong (W), paying attention to the underlined words. Correct the wrong sentences.

1. My mom saw a UFO many years ago, when she was a teenager. According to her, she saw a strange flying object in the sky one night, when going back home from a party. ☐
_____

2. There are people who say they have been abducted by ghosts and taken into their spaceships. ☐
_____

3. Zombies are people who can transform into a wolf, usually when the moon is full. ☐
_____

4 Look at the pictures and match them to their explanation.

1. He must have worn a tank top to surf.
2. It might have been a cat on the roof.
3. She might have played in the mud.
4. He simply couldn't have baked that bread himself.
5. They must have missed their dad a lot.
6. It must have stopped working.

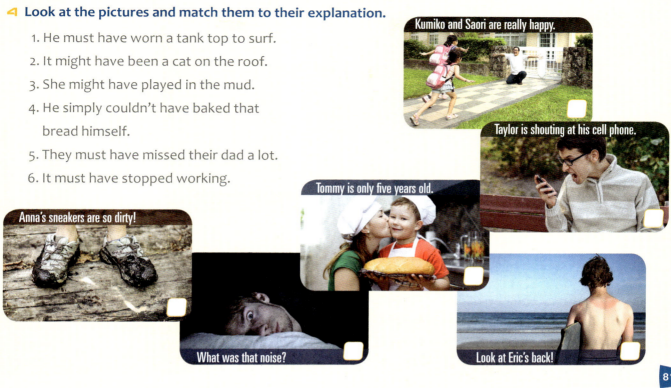

5 How certain are these sentences? Read and decide.

✓✓✓	✓✓	✓	✗	✗✗	✗✗✗
Totally possible	Not so possible	Less possible	Somewhat impossible	Likely to be impossible	Almost impossible

1. CONNOR: Alice got an A on the final test.
   KYLIE: She must have studied hard.
2. ALEX: It took them five minutes to get here from school! How were they so fast?
   MORGAN: I don't know… They simply couldn't have taken the bus or walked here…
3. MIA: Where's Lauren? She's late for the meeting.
   KEVIN: Something might have come up. I'll call her.
4. RACHEL: Look! Mom is coming back…
   JULIA: She could have forgotten something important.

6 Complete the sentences with the modal of speculation in the past and the verb in parentheses.

1. You _____ (must – see) Nick at the party last night. He was wearing a bright yellow T-shirt and a golden cap.
2. Hailey didn't go to school this morning. I guess she _____ (might – get) sick.
3. Come on, you _____ (could (not) – write) this text! It's in French, and I know you don't speak the language!
4. Alison and her sister _____ (could – make) the cake for their father's party, but it was too good, and they're terrible cooks.
5. I don't believe Eric actually saw a UFO last Sunday. The lights _____ (might – be) an aircraft or something.
6. That weird sound we heard last night _____ (must (not) – be) the wind—it was too loud.

Just for Fun

1 Use the letters to write words.

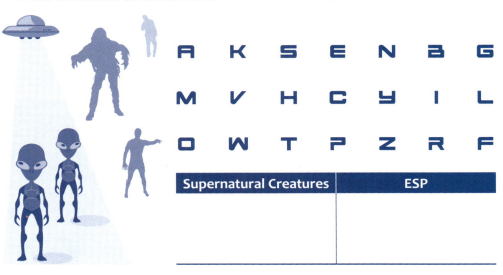

Supernatural Creatures	ESP

2 Work in pairs. How much do you know about these creatures from fiction? Do the betting quiz and find out!

> 82

	True or False?	Your Bet (1–10 Points)	Your Score
1. **Superman** is an alien who came to Earth on a spacecraft from a planet called Krypton.			
2. **Jacob,** the werewolf in the *Twilight* series, marries Bella Swan, the protagonist of the saga.			
3. In the TV series **The Walking Dead**, the world has been dominated by werewolves, and humans fight to defeat them.			
4. **Doctor Who** is an 800-year-old alien who travels in space and time on a device known as TARDIS, in a TV series of the same name.			
5. In the movie, **E.T.** uses telekinesis to make the bikes of the boys who are helping him to run away lift into the air.			
6. **Moaning Myrtle** is a ghost that haunts Hogwarts School of Witchcraft and Wizardry in Harry Potter books.			
		Final Score:	

3 Work in small groups. Invent a supernatural creature! Write a brief description below.

Name: _____

Origin: _____

Super power: _____

Physical description: _____

Personality traits: _____

4 Now share your creature with other groups. Who has the most creative profile?

What would the world be like if...?

6

Vocabulary

Milestones of the 20th Century

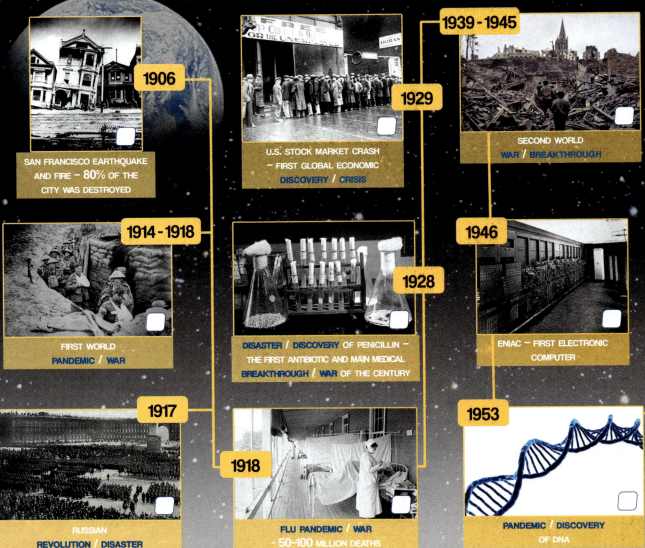

1906 — SAN FRANCISCO EARTHQUAKE AND FIRE – 80% OF THE CITY WAS DESTROYED

1929 — U.S. STOCK MARKET CRASH – FIRST GLOBAL ECONOMIC DISCOVERY / CRISIS

1939 - 1945 — SECOND WORLD WAR / BREAKTHROUGH

1914 - 1918 — FIRST WORLD PANDEMIC / WAR

1928 — DISASTER / DISCOVERY OF PENICILLIN – THE FIRST ANTIBIOTIC AND MAIN MEDICAL BREAKTHROUGH / WAR OF THE CENTURY

1946 — ENIAC – FIRST ELECTRONIC COMPUTER

1917 — RUSSIAN REVOLUTION / DISASTER

1918 — FLU PANDEMIC / WAR – 50–100 MILLION DEATHS

1953 — PANDEMIC / DISCOVERY OF DNA

---

1 Look at the timeline. Underline the correct option to complete the captions.

2 Match the sentence halves.

1. Two great wars
2. Lenin and the Bolsheviks led
3. There were few medical resources to fight
4. Sir Alexander Fleming achieved
5. In the 1930s, the world went through
6. The discovery of DNA
7. The nuclear disaster of Chernobyl

the flu pandemic, which killed millions of people.

broke out in the first half of the 20th century, in 1914 and 1939.

hit Ukraine, but it also affected other countries in Europe, in 1986.

was made by three British scientists, in 1953.

a major breakthrough with penicillin, in 1928.

the Russian Revolution in October, 1917.

its first global crisis, caused by the U.S. stock market crash.

Guess What!
When he stepped onto the lunar surface, astronaut Neil Armstrong said, "That's one small step for man; one giant leap for mankind." It became one of the most famous quotes in the world.

1962		1973		1989		1997	
CUBAN MISSILE CRISIS / DISCOVERY		FIRST CELL PHONE CALL		FALL OF THE BERLIN WALL		FIRST CLONED SHEEP – DOLLY	
	1969		1986		1990		
	FIRST MAN ON THE MOON		CHERNOBYL NUCLEAR DISASTER / BREAKTHROUGH		INVENTION OF THE WORLD WIDE WEB		

3 Complete the chart with the underlined words from Activity 2.

Verb	Noun	Verb
	a _war_	breaks out
_____	a revolution	
fight	a _____	
_____	a breakthrough	
_____	a crisis	
make	a _____	
	a _____	hits

4 🎧²² Listen to two students talking about some of the events on the timeline. Number the ones they mention.

☐ Discovery of penicillin   ☐ Invention of computers
☐ First cloned ship   ☐ First man on the moon
☐ First cell phone call   ☐ Invention of the Internet
☐ Second World War

5 Answer the questions below.

1. Why do wars break out?
   _____

2. Is the world prepared to fight a new flu pandemic? Why (not)?
   _____

3. What is the most important breakthrough of the 21st century?
   _____

4. Have you ever gone through an economic crisis in your country? How about your parents?
   _____

5. How do scientists make discoveries?
   _____

6 Share your ideas in Activity 5 with another classmate.

 Stop and Think! In your opinion, what was the most important event of the 20th century? Why?

Grammar

1 Read the article. Then read the hypothetical statements and mark (✓) what really happened.

On July 20, 1969, two astronauts, Buzz Aldrin and Neil Armstrong became the first two humans to walk on the Moon. This achievement wasn't easy—it had taken years to develop the technology they needed, and careful mathematical calculations to keep the astronauts safe. In fact, the mission was called Apollo 11 because there had been many other missions to prepare for this moment. But did you know that the Apollo 11 mission almost failed? As the astronauts descended to the Moon's surface, some alarms started going off. Fortunately, some computer programmers at Mission Control knew what was happening, and they allowed the mission to continue. Otherwise, the astronauts might have returned to Earth or crashed into the Moon. After so much work, millions of people watched on TV as humans made this great achievement.

Hypothetical
1. If people hadn't spent years developing the technology, humans wouldn't have walked on the Moon.

Reality
- ☐ a. People spent years on the technology. Humans walked on the Moon.
- ☐ b. People did not spend years on the technology. Humans didn't walk on the Moon.

Hypothetical
2. If scientists hadn't performed careful mathematical calculations, the astronauts wouldn't have been safe.

Reality
- ☐ a. Scientists performed the calculations. The astronauts were safe.
- ☐ b. Scientists did not perform the calculations. The astronauts were not safe.

Hypothetical
3. If there hadn't been many other missions, they wouldn't have been prepared.

Reality
- ☐ a. There weren't many other missions. They weren't prepared.
- ☐ b. There were many other missions. They were prepared.

Hypothetical
4. If computer programmers hadn't known what was happening, they wouldn't have let the mission continue.

Reality
- ☐ a. The programmers knew what was happening. They let the mission continue.
- ☐ b. The programmers didn't know what was happening. They didn't let the mission continue.

86

Hypothetical

5. If the astronauts had stopped their descent, they might have crashed into the Moon.

Reality

☐ a. The astronauts didn't stop their descent. They didn't crash into the Moon.
☐ b. The astronauts stopped their descent. Crashing into the Moon was a possible result.

Third Conditional

Hypothetical Past Condition	Result
If Apollo 11 hadn't been successful,	they wouldn't have landed on the Moon.
If + *subject* + *had* + *past participle*	*subject* + *would* + *have* + *present perfect*

Guess What!

Conditional sentences do not always follow a fixed template. When a sentence has characteristics of more than one type of conditional, it is called a mixed conditional: *If the astronauts had crashed into the Moon, there wouldn't be a space program now.*

2 Read and match.

1. We use the third conditional to talk about... ☐ the condition part of the sentence.
2. We use *had* and the past participle in... ☐ in place of *would* in the sentence.
3. We use *would* and the present perfect in... ☐ things that could have happened, but didn't.
4. We can also use *could* and *might*... ☐ the result part of the sentence.

3 Write the correct forms of the verbs to complete the sentences.

1. If countries _____ (not use) their resources in wars, they would have had resources to solve many social problems.
2. If James Watson hadn't discovered DNA, scientists _____ (be able) to map the human genome.
3. If scientists _____ (not map) the human genome, we wouldn't understand many genetic diseases.
4. If Alexander Fleming _____ (not discover) penicillin, we wouldn't have antibiotics.

> If Columbus hadn't come to America, Europeans wouldn't have become colonists.

⚙ **Stop and Think!** Think of some facts about the past and make some hypotheses. What could have happened if things had been different?

87

Listening and Speaking

1. **Look at the pictures. Then read the statements and circle Yes or No.**

   1. The people in the picture are in a science class.   Yes   No
   2. One of the topics of the class could be Ancient Greece.   Yes   No

2. 🎧 23 Listen to the beginning of one of Professor Gardner's classes. Is he going to talk about a real war? Discuss with a partner.

3. 🎧 24 One of the students in Professor Gardner's class is taking notes. Listen to another excerpt of the class and number the notes in the order the ideas are mentioned.

Soviet Union → occupied countries in Eastern Europe → control the world? ☐

U.S. → against communism
vs.
Soviet Union → U.S. took too long to enter WW II → millions of Russians died ☐

Hostile relationship → arms race → ATOMIC AGE ☐

Cuban Missile Crisis: Soviets wanted to install nukes in Cuba (1962) → almost ended in WW III ☐

U.S. + Russia → allies during WW II ☐

U.S. → interference in other countries ↘ accumulation of nuclear weapons ☐

After WW II → rivalry ↘ distrust ☐

Glossary
ally: a country that agrees to support another during a war
rivalry: a situation of unfriendly competition
arms race: a competition between two countries to have superiority in the development and accumulation of nuclear weapons
nuke: a nuclear weapon

> **Guess What!**
> The Cuban Missile Crisis, which took place in October, 1962, was the most tense period of the Cold War. Fortunately, the United States and the Soviet Union reached an agreement: the Russians agreed to take their nuclear weapon off Cuba and the Americans promised not to invade the Caribbean island.

4 🎧²⁴ **Listen to the class once more. Write F if the statement represents a fact and O if it represents an opinion.**

1. If the Cold War had actually happened, the world would have been destroyed. _____
2. The United States and the Soviet Union were allies during the Second World War, but became enemies after its end. _____
3. Millions of Soviets wouldn't have died if the United States had entered the Second World War earlier. _____
4. The Russians wanted to control the world. _____
5. If the Russians had insisted on installing nuclear weapons in Cuba, a Third World War would have started. _____

5 **You are going to discuss an issue in groups. Follow the steps below.**

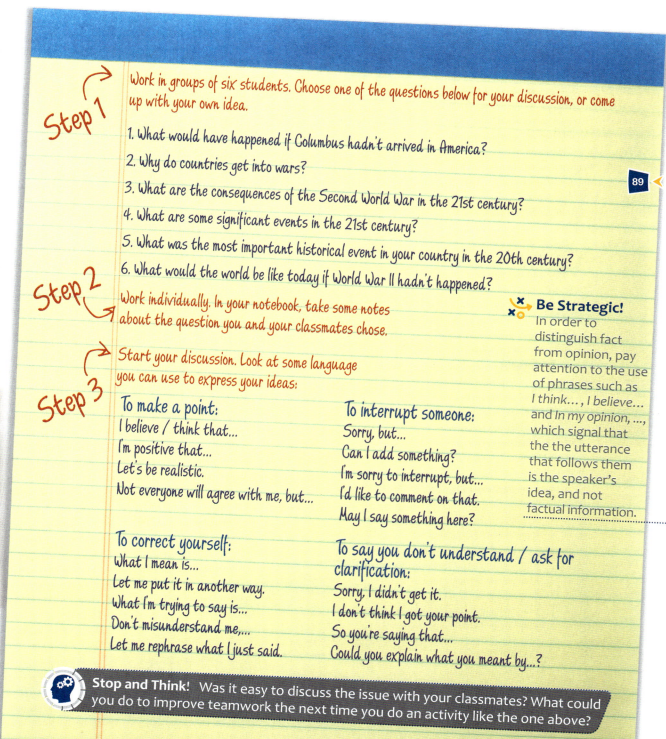

Step 1: Work in groups of six students. Choose one of the questions below for your discussion, or come up with your own idea.

1. What would have happened if Columbus hadn't arrived in America?
2. Why do countries get into wars?
3. What are the consequences of the Second World War in the 21st century?
4. What are some significant events in the 21st century?
5. What was the most important historical event in your country in the 20th century?
6. What would the world be like today if World War II hadn't happened?

Step 2: Work individually. In your notebook, take some notes about the question you and your classmates chose.

Step 3: Start your discussion. Look at some language you can use to express your ideas:

To make a point:
I believe / think that...
I'm positive that...
Let's be realistic.
Not everyone will agree with me, but...

To interrupt someone:
Sorry, but...
Can I add something?
I'm sorry to interrupt, but...
I'd like to comment on that.
May I say something here?

To correct yourself:
What I mean is...
Let me put it in another way.
What I'm trying to say is...
Don't misunderstand me,...
Let me rephrase what I just said.

To say you don't understand / ask for clarification:
Sorry, I didn't get it.
I don't think I got your point.
So you're saying that...
Could you explain what you meant by...?

Be Strategic! In order to distinguish fact from opinion, pay attention to the use of phrases such as *I think...*, *I believe...* and *In my opinion, ...*, which signal that the the utterance that follows them is the speaker's idea, and not factual information.

Stop and Think! Was it easy to discuss the issue with your classmates? What could you do to improve teamwork the next time you do an activity like the one above?

2 Read an extract from an e-book about the Portuguese discoveries. Check if any of your ideas from Activity 1 are mentioned.

Chapter 15 – The Portuguese and Their Discoveries

In the 15th and 16th centuries, the Portuguese set out to explore and conquer new territories, which led them to make significant discoveries in the Americas, Africa and Asia. They also traced important maritime routes and mapped the coasts of several countries. The Portuguese were so powerful and skilled that in less than a century, their empire had extended to four different continents.

The Portuguese expansion started in 1419, with several expeditions mapping the coast of West Africa. After that, the Portuguese set several exploration milestones:

1489 Bartolomeu Dias reached the **Cape of Good Hope** (in today's _____) and entered the Indian Ocean.

1498 **Vasco da Gama** sailed along the coast of Africa to reach India, setting out a **trade** _____ between India and Portugal.

1500 Pedro Alvares Cabral landed in **Brazil** and claimed the territory for _____.

1506 Tristao da Cunha **made landfall** on **Madagascar**, an island off of the east coast of _____.

1510 Alfonso de Albuquerque conquered Goa, an important city in _____.

1511 Alfonso de Albuquerque conquered **Malacca**, a major trade _____ in Malaysia.

1513 Jorge Alvares reached China and established _____ with the Chinese.

1521 Cristovao de Mendonca discovered _____.

1530 _____, King of Portugal, began the colonization of Brazil.

1557 The Portuguese settled permanently in **Macau**, a _____ territory.

3 🎧 25 Listen to a recording of the book chapter in Activity 2. Complete the timeline with the words in the box.

> Africa   Australia   Chinese   India   John III
> port   Portugal   route   South Africa   trade

Stop and Think! Do you know any famous explorers from other countries? If you do, what can you say about them?

Glossary

trade: the activity of buying and selling goods between countries

make landfall: arrive at a piece of land after a long journey by sea or air

① dn DailyNews

② **Local News** | World | Sports | Opin

③ December 22, 2047

Weather

 Now 23°C

 Tonight 14°C

 Tomorrow 18°C – 22°C

④

⑤ **UN Member States Sign World Peace Treaty in NY**

⑥ 193 countries sign historical document to end all wars at UN headquarters

New Pictures of First Human Mission on Mars Revealed by NASA

Dr. Indra Bhat Confirms Cure for All Types of Cancer

Indian scientist made announcement during WHO Cancer Conference

After 20 Years of Hard Efforts, Global Warming Finally Revertsed, Say Studies

⑦ **EU Economy**
2047 will be the best year for EU countries' economies

New York 2048
The Big Apple is almost ready for its first Olympic Games

AI is Now Real
First intelligent computer, Deep Pink, is everyone's Christmas wish

---

1 Look at the front page of an online newspaper. Match the sections to the descriptions below.

☐ Other news are presented in this section.

☐ Real-time information about the weather and a forecast are usually presented in one of the corners of the page.

☐ The newspaper's name is called the **nameplate**. It can be accompanied by a logo.

☐ The story printed in larger font, accompanied by the biggest picture, is the **lead story**—the most important at the time. The higher a story is on the home page, the more important it is.

☐ The **subhead** provides further information about the news story. Its font is smaller than the headline's.

☐ The **top menu** presents the main sections of the online newspaper. Remaining sections might be presented at the bottom of the page.

☐ The **headline** summarizes the story, in order to encourage readers to click on it and read the full text. The bigger the headline, the more important the story is.

| Culture | Economy | Lifestyle | Tech | Health | Travel |

Sign in

2 Answer the questions about the front page.

1. Is it a real front page? How do you know that?
   _____.

2. What do all the headlines have in common?
   _____.

3. Is it possible to look for news stories on the newspaper's website? If so, how?
   _____.

3 Work in small groups. You and your classmates are going to prepare the home page of an online newspaper for a future date. Follow the steps below.

STEP 1 Choose a name for your newspaper and design a logo—they will be your newspaper's nameplate.

STEP 2 Choose a month, day and year for your newspaper. Are you going to set it in the near future or in a distant year?

STEP 3 Think of the sections your online newspaper will have. They will be set on a menu at the top of the page.

STEP 4 Imagine the news stories your home page will present. Consider the questions below.
• Are you presenting positive or negative news stories? Or a mix of both?
• Have you considered what would have happened if something else had not? How would it affect the events of your news story?
• What images will you use to illustrate these stories?
• Are your news stories varied? Do they cover most of the sections of your newspaper?
• Which story will be the lead story?

STEP 5 Now that you have chosen the stories, write the headlines and the subheads. Keep the tips below in mind.
• Summarize the story in the headline, in an attractive way.
• Use the present tense, with active but short verbs.
• The subhead should provide further information about the story.

STEP 6 Lay out your newspaper home page. You can use one of the options below:
• A free website builder service.
• A slide show presentation program.
• A word processor program.
• A large sheet of paper and colored markers.

4 Share your newspaper home page with other groups.

Stop and Think! Which newspaper home page was the most interesting? Why?

Review

1 Mark (✓) the correct alternative to complete the sentences. Pay attention to the words in bold.

1. The scientists _____ a major **breakthrough** in the fight against cancer with the new drug.
   ☐ have gone through   ☐ achieved   ☐ have hit

2. After _____ the worst economic **crisis** in its history, the country is gradually recovering.
   ☐ having gone through   ☐ making   ☐ breaking out

3. Although the two countries are trying to reach an agreement about their border, analysts think a **war** _____.
   ☐ will fight   ☐ will lead   ☐ will break out

4. The Portuguese and the Spaniards _____ important territory **discoveries** in the 15th and 16th centuries.
   ☐ made   ☐ achieved   ☐ went through

5. Simón Bolivar _____ **revolutions** for the independence of Bolivia, Colombia, Ecuador, Panama and Venezuela in the 19th century.
   ☐ hit   ☐ broke out   ☐ led

6. Several international health organizations are worried about how to _____ a future flu **pandemic**.
   ☐ lead   ☐ fight   ☐ make

7. What was the worst natural **disaster** that _____ your country?
   ☐ has ever hit   ☐ has ever made   ☐ has ever achieved

2 Complete the sentences with a collocation from the box. Pay attention to the verb form.

> make / discovery   fight / pandemic   disaster / hit   achieve / breakthrough

1. In 2012, scientists at CERN _____ a _____ that changed the history of physics with the finding of the Higgs boson, an elementary particle.

2. The computer industry _____ an important _____ with the invention of the chip in the 1950s.

3. The 2010 earthquake in Haiti was a terrible natural _____ that _____ the small Caribbean island and killed over 220,000 people.

4. Do you think the world is ready to _____ a new _____ ?

3 Match the sentences in Activity 2 to the pictures below.

4 **Are the sentences correct (C) or incorrect (I)? Correct the incorrect sentences.**

1. If I had called my parents about my delay last night, they wouldn't be angry at me today.
   _____

2. I wouldn't have heard about the Cuban Missile crisis if I haven't learned about it in class.
   _____

3. Would we have any freedom of speech today if the Nazis had win WW II?
   _____

4. If I had left home earlier, I wouldn't be late for Mr. Gardner's class. I need to run now!
   _____

5. The war wouldn't have broken out if the president hadn't been assassinated.
   _____

6. My country would have been in a better economic situation now if we hadn't gone through a crisis in 2014.
   _____

5 **Use the prompts and the images to write conditional sentences.**

0

Mark / be 18 years / fight in the Second World War *If Mark hadn't been 18 years old, he wouldn't have fought in the Second World War.*

1

he / fight in WW II / go to France
_____
_____
_____

2

he / go to France / meet Marie
_____
_____
_____

3

Mark and Marie / meet / get married
_____
_____
_____

4

they / meet and get married / have my grandpa, James
_____
_____
_____

5

my grandpa / be born / I / be here in France today!
_____
_____
_____

Just for Fun

1 Unscramble the words to complete the crossword puzzle. What is the mystery word?

1. In 79 AD, a volcano eruption destroyed Pompeii, an ancient Greek city. The eruption was the most famous natural SATDESIR of the ancient world.
2. The Tulip Mania in the 17th century was the first widely documented economic SSIIRC. It happened due to the speculative rise and fall in the prices of tulip bulbs, taking the stock market to a collapse.
3. The Justinian Plague, which began in 541 AD, was the first MDACENPI known in history. It was caused by a bacteria called *Yersinia pestis*, transmitted to humans by fleas.
4. The American LNROEIVTOU, which took place between 1965 and 1983, eventually led to the independence of the thirteen American colonies and the foundation of the United States.
5. Charles Darwin's theory of evolution, published in his book *On the Origin of Species*, was a major BHRGTARUEKHO in biology, changing the way we saw the development of life on our planet.
6. The first RWA recorded in history happened in Mesopotomia, in 2700 BC, between two peoples: the Sumerians and the Elamites.

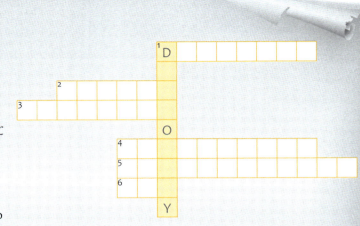

2 Work with a partner. Two of the statements in Activity 1 present incorrect information. Which are they? How many points would you bet on your answer?

	1	2	3	4	5	6
Incorrect answer:						
Your bet (1–10 points):						

3 Help the letters fall into the correct position to create a quote. Who said it?

1 Read Katie's entries in her diary. Match the actions involved in Katie's arrangements and plans to study abroad.

1. apply for
2. buy
3. choose
4. enroll
5. get
6. make

☐ local food
☐ a student visa
☐ a passport
☐ in local events
☐ travel insurance
☐ new friends

7. participate
8. take out
9. try
10. fill out
11. make

☐ plane tickets
☐ a language school
☐ in a course
☐ travel arrangements
☐ forms

Dear Diary,

Finally one of my dreams is going to come true! I'm going to learn French in Provence. I'll tell you all about it here!

Mar 12

I've **gotten my passport** today and finally **chosen the language school!** I'm going to study at French +, an institute in Aix-en-Provence. I've sent them an email asking for info to **enroll in their summer course**. Hope they answer it soon...

Mar 21

It's Sunday evening. I've spent the weekend **filling out forms** and gathering documents to **apply for a student visa**. I'm so excited about all this! Mom says she'll miss me—I'll miss her, too!

Apr 12

Mom and I went online tonight and **made my final travel arrangements** together. We've **bought the plane tickets, took out travel insurance** and wrote an email to my host mother, Mme. Dubois. She answered it right away in perfect English. She seems to be very friendly!

List of things I'd like to do while in Provence

- learn French (of course!)
- spend a weekend in Paris (check if French + promotes students' trips)
- participate in local events (parade on Bastille Day – Jul 14)
- try local food
- make new friends!!!

98

2 🎧²⁶ **Listen to Katie talking to a friend about her plans to study abroad. When did the conversation probably take place?**

Before April 12 ☐   After April 12 ☐

3 **Complete the questions. Then answer them.**

1. If you were planning to study abroad, what would you do first—get a _____ or choose a _____?
   _____

2. What would you need to do before enrolling in a _____ abroad, if you decided to learn a foreign language in another country?
   _____

3. Is it important to take out _____ when studying abroad? Why or why not?
   _____

4. Besides participating in _____, what can a foreign student do to learn about the culture of the country he / she is studying in?
   _____

4 Work in small groups. Share your answers in Activity 3 with your classmates.

Guess What!
The country that currently sends the highest number of students abroad is China. In 2014, 459,800 Chinese students studied in another country. Their favorite destination is the United States.

Stop and Think! Is there anything else Katie should do before traveling to France?

Grammar

1 Read the conversation. Jake makes one mistake when talking about Katie's plans. What is it? Go back to pages 98 and 99 if necessary.

- Hi Jake! How are things with Katie?
  - Hi Emily. Things with Katie… Well… She's going away for the summer.
- Really?
  - Yeah. She said she will study French in Paris.
- Oh, Jake… I'm sorry for you.
  - Please don't be. I'll be OK.
- But did you talk to her about your feelings?
  - No, I didn't. There was no time! I told her I'm going to get a new car in the summer, though, but she didn't care!
- Jake, you're so silly sometimes… You must say you like her! What are you going to do now?
  - I might have a chance this afternoon. Katie said she hasn't gotten a visa yet, and she invited me to go to the French consulate with her after school.
- That's great!
  - Yeah… but she said she wants to discuss the history project on the way. She has no feelings for me.
- Jake, if you don't tell her how you feel, I will!
  - OK, OK… I'll talk to her.

Reported Speech

Direct:	Reported:
"She's going **away** for the summer" — *Present continuous*	Jake **said** (that) Katie **was going away** for the summer. — *Past continuous*
"I'm sorry for you." — *Present of be*	Emily **told** Jake (that) she **was** sorry for him. — *Past of be*
"Please **don't be**." — *Imperative*	Jake **asked** Emily **not to be** sorry for him. — *Infinitive*
"**Did** you **talk** to her about your feelings?" — *Simple past*	Emily **asked** if Jake **had talked** to Katie about his feelings. — *Past perfect*

In **reported statements**, the change in the verb tense is optional when:
- the event/action is still true at the moment of speaking.
- it is a general truth.
- the direct statement has just been said.

> 100

2 Underline examples of reported speech in Activity 1.

3 Complete with the correct words. Change verb tenses.
1. **Jake:** Is it true you're going to France this summer?
   Jake asked Katie if it _____ true she _____ to France the following summer.
2. **Katie:** Your parents don't even allow you to go to school by yourself.
   Katie said Jake's parents _____ even _____ _____ to go to school by _____.
3. **Jake:** Have you chosen the language school yet?
   Jake _____ Katie _____ she _____ already _____ the language school.
4. **Katie:** I asked the school to help me take out insurance, but they haven't answered yet. Katie _____ she _____ _____ the school to help her take out insurance, but that they _____ _____ yet.

4 Report the statements below.

1. How are things with Katie?
   _____

2. You must say you like her!
   _____

3. _____
   She has no feelings for me.

4. If you don't tell her how you feel, I will!
   _____

5 🎧²⁷ Now listen to Jake talking to Katie after school. Report two things they each said.

Jake	Katie

6 **Think Fast!** Work with a partner. Report an imaginary conversation between Jake and Katie in which he really tells her how he feels.

Reading and Writing

1 Look at the text and pictures. Underline the option that describes what kind of text it is.

1. It's a brochure about regular university courses for foreign students.
2. It's a leaflet to promote study programs in other countries.

Go Beyond with GU Abroad Programs!

Globe University undergraduates have access to study abroad programs all over the world.

Have you gotten your passport? Apply for a student visa now and study abroad! Studying in another country is a life-changing experience! You meet people from other cultures, learn their customs and language and make new friends! It's an experience that **boosts** your decision-making skills and self-confidence, helping you become a flexible and open-minded young adult, ready for the challenges of academic and professional life.

At Globe University, we offer undergraduates three types of exchange programs:

- **Semester Abroad with Globe University** — a fully-accredited academic semester in your **major** at one of our affiliates in any of these countries: Mexico, Costa Rica, Brazil, Colombia, Argentina, France, Spain, Germany, South Africa, India, China, Japan or Australia.

Globe University undergraduates with fellow Chinese students at an affiliate college in Shanghai.

- **Summer Abroad with Globe University** — a 12-week program with extended studies in your major and an intensive language—learning program in any of these countries: Mexico, France, Spain, Germany, Italy, Russia, China and Japan.

- **Semester OnBoard with Globe University** — A 20-week program on MS Global, the university cruise ship, visiting 13 cities in 11 countries. Students attend regular, fully-accredited GU courses aboard, while engaging in field trips and classes at local affiliates.

 NEW

All the programs have an exciting social program, which includes short weekend trips, city tours and parties!

In order to join any of the programs, you must:
- Have a minimum 3.5 **GPA** (out of 5.0)
- Be currently enrolled for the semester
- Have completed 16 **credit** hours at GU

Enroll now! For further information, visit the Academic Advisory Office in the Atlas Building, or schedule an appointment with Ms. Anna Watson, Senior Academic Advisor, by WhatsApp – 555-908-9876.

www.globeuniversity.edu

2 Read the leaflet. Mark (✓) YES, NO or *NOT MENTIONED* for the statements below.

According to the leaflet, …	YES	NO	NOT MENTIONED
1. studying in another country can change students' lives.			
2. students who study abroad become more extroverted.			
3. students who go to France for the summer program stay in Paris.			
4. there aren't countries from the southern hemisphere in the summer program.			
5. *MS Global* takes students to 11 different countries in 20 weeks.			
6. entertainment is not part of the study abroad programs offered by GU.			
7. students who have low grades can still participate in the programs.			
8. students who have just entered Globe University can join any of the programs.			

3 Think Fast! How many different countries are mentioned in the leaflet?

4 Look at the leaflet again. Read the sentences below and write *T* (True) or *F* (False).

1. Use of different font and font sizes _____
2. Long paragraphs _____
3. Text organized into bullet points _____
4. Use of images to attract readers _____
5. Language is formal and academic _____
6. Language is objective, but persuasive _____

Be Strategic!
When writing a text, it is vital to identify the possible readers—the audience. Even if people won't read it in real life, knowing who these possible readers are help you define several aspects of your text.

103

5 Work with a partner. Create a leaflet for a fictitious study program. Follow the steps below.

Step 1 Choose the type of program you want to create the leaflet for. Look at some options:
- A work-and-study program abroad
- A study-on-board program
- A summer language learning program
- A full academic semester program
- Other: _____

Step 2 Consider the audience you are going to write for—who would be interested in the program on your leaflet?

Step 3 In your notebook, write a first version of your leaflet.
- Try to be persuasive, but concise. You can use adjectives and benefits of the program to convince your readers.
- Make sure to include all the necessary information—don't forget to mention how people can learn more about it.

Step 4 Think of images you can use to illustrate your leaflet. Also, consider the use of colors, fonts and other graphic elements to make your leaflet more attractive for readers.

Step 5 Now create your leaflet on a separate sheet of paper. Keep in mind the features in Activity 4.

Step 6 Once your leaflet is ready, post it on the classroom wall.

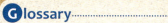

Glossary

boost: help something to increase or become better

major: a student's main subject at college or university

GPA: grade point average (the average of a student's grade over a period of time)

credit: a part of a course in a college or university completed successfully

Stop and Think! Read your classmates' leaflets. Which of the study programs advertised would you like to attend? Why?

Culture

1 Look at the pictures in the magazine. Match them to the captions.

Study and Have Fun in Ireland!

Over 120,000 international students chose Ireland as their academic destination in 2015. Why don't you join them? Take a look at some of the country's attractions.

1. Galway, a city on the western coast of Ireland, is famous for its many cultural festivals throughout the year. Come and participate in the local events!

2. The **Cliffs** of Moher rise 120 meters above the sea and offer one of the most breathtaking views of the country.

3. Blackrock castle and observatory, in Cork, located in the south coast of Ireland.

4. One of the buildings of Trinity College, the oldest university in the country, founded in 1592.

5. Try the local food, like the Irish stew made with lamb, potatoes, carrots and herbs.

2 ⁿ²⁸ Listen to an education agent talking with two students about studying in Ireland. Mark (✓) the advantages of studying in the country.

1. Ireland is closer to the students' home country than the UK. ☐
2. There are several high-quality colleges, institutes of technology and universities in Ireland. ☐
3. Dublin is more interesting than any major British city. ☐
4. Studying in Ireland would cost less than studying in the UK. ☐
5. People can attend art festivals in Ireland. ☐
6. Irish cities are modern, with high-tech buildings only. ☐
7. There are extremely beautiful cliffs, places by the sea and also in the countryside. ☐

Stop and Think! Which is the oldest university in your country?

3 Answer the questions. Then share your answers with the class.

1. Based on the information you have, would you like to live and study in Ireland? Why or why not?
_____

2. Which other country would you choose to study abroad? Why?
_____

3. What do you know about the advantages of studying in that country?
_____

4 Think Fast! Which places on the brochure are mentioned in the conversation?

Glossary
cliff: a high, steep surface of a rock or mountain

Project

1 Look at a page of a website with information for foreigners who want to study in the United States. How many sections are there on the website?

Getting a Student Visa   College Application   Financial Aid   F.A.Q.

3 Answer the questions below. Then discuss your ideas with your classmates.

1. Which information on the webpage is the most useful?

_____
_____

2. Would any information be different for your country? If so, how?

_____
_____

3. What other items could be included in the section "Student Life in the US"?

_____
_____

4 Work in small groups. Prepare a section of an online guide for foreign students coming to a college or university in your country. Follow the steps below.

Step 1 Choose the section of the guide you are going to write. Use the sections on the website on pages 106 and 107 for ideas.

Step 2 Collect information for the section that would be useful to international students. You can search online, call or visit colleges and universities that accept foreign students in your country.

Step 3 Once you have the information, organize it into paragraphs. Try to be clear and concise—remember the students reading the information might not be fluent in English.

Step 4 Select images to illustrate the information.

Step 5 Write a final version of your guide section.

5 Share your section of the guide for international students with other groups.

Stop and Think! How could the information collected by your group and others be shared with real students coming to your country?

Review

1 Complete the crossword puzzle. Use the sentences as clues.

Across →

1. What are the documents needed to _____ a passport?
4. When are you going to _____ in the summer program?
5. Be sure you have a visa in order to _____ the travel arrangements.
7. Check the city calendar to know if you'll be able to _____ in a local event.
9. Katie needs her mother's credit card to _____ the plane tickets to France.

Down ↓

2. Do you know where I can go to _____ out travel insurance?
3. I'm talking to former students so that I can _____ the best college abroad.
6. If you really want to study Spanish in Spain this summer, you need to _____ for a visa now!
8. I'm not sure if I'll _____ the local food when I travel to Korea. I'm a picky eater, you know…

2 Use the collocations from Activity 1 to label the pictures.

3 Read the direct speech statements. Then mark (✓) the correct reported version.

1. **LEAH:** "I'm not going to study abroad this summer."
   Leah said she wasn't going to study abroad that summer. ☐
   Leah said I wasn't going to study abroad this summer. ☐

2. **ETHAN:** "Do I need a student visa to study in Ireland?"
   Ethan said I needed a student vista to study in Ireland? ☐
   Ethan asked if he needed a student vista to study in Ireland. ☐

3. **MR. THOMPSON:** "You must enroll for the course now, Mia."
   Mia's teacher said Mia she must enroll for the course now. ☐
   Mia's teacher told her she had to enroll for the course then. ☐

4. **JOHN:** "How did you like the food in Peru, Kayla?"
   John asked Kayla how she had liked the local food in Peru. ☐
   John asked Kayla if she liked the local food in Peru. ☐

5. **CLERK:** "Please fill out this form to get the passport, Ms. Taylor."
   The clerk told Ms. Taylor to fill out that form to get the passport. ☐
   The clerk said please filled out this form to get the passport. ☐

6. **LAUREN:** "Have you made all the arrangements for your trip, Dave?"
   Lauren asked Dave if he had made all the arrangements for his trip. ☐
   Lauren asked Dave he made all the arrangements for his trip. ☐

4 Complete the reported statements with the correct verb form, changing the tense.

1. **OLIVIA:** "I'm so excited about my trip to Japan!"
   Olivia said she _____ excited about her trip to Japan.

2. **DYLAN:** "My sister **is studying** in Australia this year."
   Dylan said his sister _____ in Australia that year.

3. **BRIANNA:** "**There are** five exchange students in my school."
   Brianna said _____ five exchange students in her class.

4. **WILL:** "**Are** you **going** to study a semester abroad, Andy?"
   Will asked Andy if he _____ to study a semester abroad.

5. **ALYSSA:** "Who **told** you about this school in Provence, Katie?"
   Alyssa asked Katie who _____ her about that school in Provence.

6. **SOPHIA:** "Where **will** you **stay** if you **decide** to learn German in Berlin, Emma?"
   Sophia asked Emma where she _____ if she _____ to learn German in Berlin.

5 Collect direct quotes from the people below. Then report them.

1. Something your teacher said: "_____"
   Reported speech: _____

2. Something a friend said: "_____"
   Reported speech: _____

3. Something a person in your family said: "_____"
   Reported speech: _____

Just for Fun

1 Complete the double cryptogram.

1. Apply for a student			I							
			6	5	17	7				
2. B U		L	A			C				
15	23	8	1	7	19	20	22	5	18	20	22	17
3. Choose a			U			C				
	1	7	19	13	7	13	20	17	14	16	16	1
4. Enroll in a	C	U								
		16	21	17	20					
5. Make		F		N						
19	20	4	21	5	20	19	12	17		

" _ E _ _ L _ _ _ _ , "
22 14 20 — 4 16 21 1 12 — 5 17 — 7 — 15 16 16 18

_ _ _ O _ _ _ _ _ _ _
7 19 12 — 22 14 16 17 20 — 4 14 16 — 12 16 — 19 16 22

R _ _ _ _ _ _ _ _ _ _ _ _ ."
22 21 7 6 20 1 — 21 20 7 12 — 16 19 1 23 — 7 — 8 7 13 20

Saint Augustine

 2 Play tic-tac-toe with a classmate. Create reported statements or questions.

SAID	SUGGESTED	TOLD
INVITED	**CHOOSE THE VERB!**	ASKED
EXPLAINED	ANSWERED	WARNED

3 Write five words from the Culture section in the grid. Then play battleships with a classmate!

	A	B	C	D	E	F	G	H	I	J
1										
2										
3										
4										
5										
6										
7										
8										
9										
10										

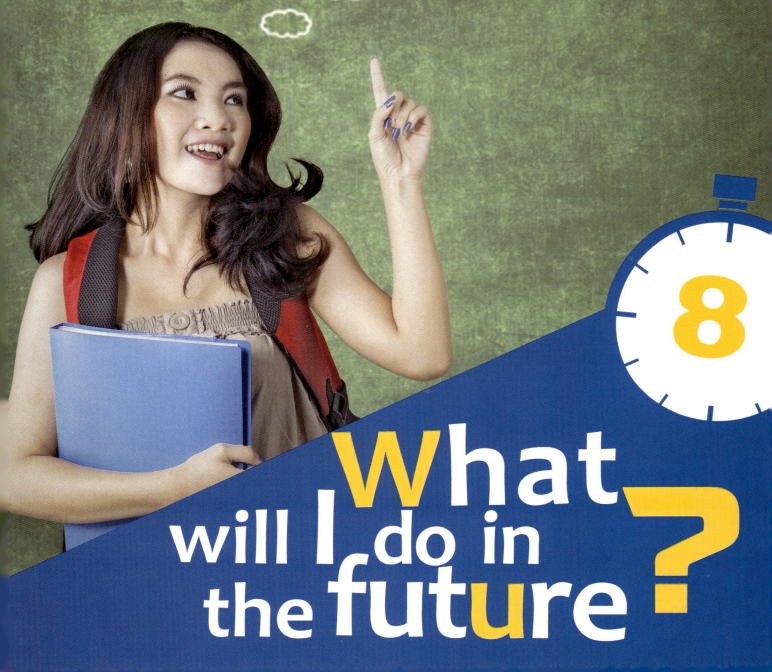

8
What will I do in the future?

Vocabulary

1 Read the text on the computer screen. What is Mackenzie doing?

 112

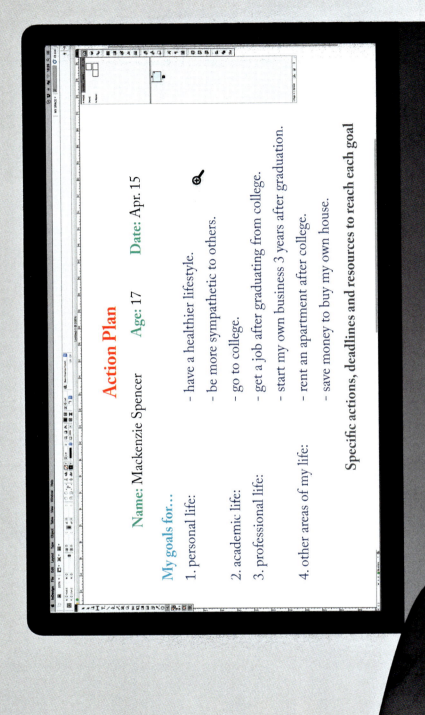

Action Plan

Name: Mackenzie Spencer   **Age:** 17   **Date:** Apr. 15

My goals for…

1. personal life:
 - have a healthier lifestyle.
 - be more sympathetic to others.

2. academic life:
 - go to college.

3. professional life:
 - get a job after graduating from college.
 - start my own business 3 years after graduation.

4. other areas of my life:
 - rent an apartment after college.
 - save money to buy my own house.

Specific actions, deadlines and resources to reach each goal

2 Add words from the text to complete the collocations in the chart. Not all of them will be completed now.

3 Add the phrases from the box to the chart in Activity 2 to form new collocations.

to vocational school

doing physical activities   resources, like water
patient with my little sister   a car
a gap year   around the world
married   a less stressful routine

1. have	
2. be	
3. go	
4. get	
5. start	
6. rent	
7. save	
8. take	
9. travel	
10. buy	

4 Complete the statements and questions.

1. Is it a good idea to _____ a gap year after high school?
2. Some people prefer to _____ to a vocational school instead of going to college. What do you think about it?
3. What should young people do to _____ a less stressful routine?
4. How can a person _____ more patient with others?
5. Is it easy for a sedentary teenager to _____ doing physical activities?
6. If a young person is studying in a college out of his / her town, is it better to _____ an apartment or to live in a dorm on campus?
7. When is it better to _____ a job? After graduating from college or while still in college?
8. Which is more important? Saving money to _____ a house or to _____ a car?
9. Some young people _____ married right after going to college. How do you feel about it?
10. What skills does a young person who wants to _____ his / her own business need to have?

5 Work in small groups. Choose four questions from Activity 4. Share your answers.

 Stop and Think!: Do you think writing an action plan is a good idea? Why (not)?

Guess What!
An action plan is a document that shows your goals for the future, as well as the steps and resources you need to take to achieve them. Also, the deadlines for the goals and steps are set in the plan.

113

Grammar

1 Read the conversation. What is Mackenzie writing about?

CAMERON: What are you doing, Mackenzie?

MACKENZIE: I'm writing an action plan with my future goals…

CAMERON: Really? How interesting! I've written mine already.

MACKENZIE: How nice! So you can help me! In the third part of the plan, I need to say where I see myself in ten years.

CAMERON: Well, I'll be working as a wildlife photographer in Africa. I'll be living in my own house in Kenya, Tanzania or South Africa. I won't be married, that's for sure!

MACKENZIE: Wow! Your goals are amazing! And how are you going to reach them?

CAMERON: This time next year, I'll be studying photography at the Arts University. I was already accepted!

MACKENZIE: Congrats! You're a great photographer…

CAMERON: And you, Mackenzie? What are your plans? Where do you see yourself in ten years?

MACKENZIE: Hmm… I won't be working for a company, that's all I know… I want to have my own business. But I can't make up my mind.

CAMERON: You're a great cook! There are several gastronomy programs at different universities…

MACKENZIE: That sounds awesome! Why didn't I think about it before? I'll open a restaurant! It'll be "Mack's Kitchen"!

CAMERON: In ten years, you will be running the kitchen of your own restaurant! And I'll be visiting you when I come to the States on vacation!

Future continuous

| In ten years, | Cameron **will** | be | working in Africa. |
| Mackenzie **won't** | be | working for a company. |

will/won't + be + v-ing

Now ——————————— Ten years later

2 Circle examples of the future continuous in Activity 1.

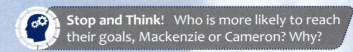
Stop and Think! Who is more likely to reach their goals, Mackenzie or Cameron? Why?

3 Read a letter another student wrote to her "future self." Fill in the gaps with the future continuous forms of the verbs in parentheses.

Dear future me,

I hope you get this letter, written fifteen years before. I hope you're a nice, healthy and reliable adult woman. I hope you (1) _____ (work) at a big hospital, as a doctor, as it is my dream today. If everything goes according to plan, you (2) _____ (treat) children as a pediatrician. You will be married to Mr. Right and (3) _____ (take care) of your own children—preferably a boy and a girl. You (4) _____ (live) at a nice, comfortable house, not too far from your parents'. You (5) _____ (see) mom and dad frequently, and they (6) _____ (enjoy) their grandchildren. You (7) _____ (travel) abroad at least once a year—sometimes without the kids! You (8) _____ still _____ (spend) time with your BFFs from high school, Anna and Chloe. And you (9) _____ still _____ (laugh) at the same things.

All in all, I hope you'll be happy. Even if none of the above ever comes true!

Yours truly,

Morgan

4 Write sentences in the future continuous to express the plans below. Use the prompts.

1. Kevin is studying engineering in college. He is going to graduate in three years' time.
   (In three years' time / work / engineer)
   _____

2. Savannah is learning Spanish. She is going to finish her course in Spain next year.
   (Next year / live and study / Spain)
   _____

3. Our teacher is going to work in another school next semester.
   (Next semester / teach / our class anymore)
   _____

4. My best friend will go to a college in another state after summer.
   (After summer / see / my friend every day)
   _____

5 What are your plans? Write about yourself.

1. Next weekend, I'll be _____
2. Next month, I'll _____
3. During my next vacation, _____
4. This time next year, _____

Listening and Speaking

1 Look at the picture. What can you infer about the situation? Underline the correct answers.

By Sean Hopkins

Subject: Career Development

Teacher: Mr. Roberts

1. Who is Mr. Roberts?
   - Person #1
   - Person #2
   - Person #3

2. What is the student going to talk about?
   a) How important having a career in CS is.
   b) Work areas and possibilities in CS.
   c) Why he chose CS as his major in college.

2 🎧²⁹ Listen to Sean. Complete the statements below. Your inferences in Activity 1 will help you.

1. Sean's presentation is divided into _____ parts.
2. In one of the sections, he's going to talk about _____ and colleges where people can _____ computer science.
3. Artificial Intelligence is not a _____ area of study in computer science.
4. A student asked Sean a question about an _____ of _____ in computer science.

> **Be Strategic!**
> Besides using "hints" from the text, you can use your knowledge of the world to infer information while listening. In Activity 1, for example, it is expected that the the presenter—in this case, the student, stands up, while the teacher remains seated at the front of the class.

3 🎧²⁹ Listen to Sean again. What can you infer about him, his presentation and one of his classmates? Circle *T (True)* or *F (False)*.

1. Sean didn't organize his presentation very well.   T   F
2. Sean is a good presenter who cares about his audience.   T   F
3. One of Sean's classmates was not paying attention to the presentation.   T   F
4. Sean's classmate was respectful to him and polite.   T   F
5. Sean's visuals are connected to what he's saying.   T   F

4 Look at some signposting language used in presentations. Organize the items in the chart.

a) As you can see on this slide, …
b) Do you have any questions?
c) First, I'll…
d) Good morning, everyone!
e) Hi, guys!
f) I think we can conclude from my presentation that…
g) If you have any questions, I'll be happy to answer them now.
h) Last of all, I'll…
i) Let me outline the structure of my presentation.
j) Next, I'll…
k) OK. So let's start by looking at…
l) On the slide, there's…
m) Please take a look at this…
n) Secondly, I'll…
o) Thank you for listening.
p) Thanks for your attention.

Greeting Your Audience	Outlining the Presentation
e	
Starting a Topic	**Referring to Your Visuals**
c	
Inviting Questions	**Ending Your Presentation and Thanking the Audience**

5 Now prepare a presentation on a college major. Follow the steps below.

Steps

1. Choose a major for your presentation.
2. Outline the structure of the presentation. What aspects of the major would you like to talk about?
3. Do some research and collect information.
4. Use a slide presentation program to organize the information into a presentation—don't forget to include attractive visuals!
5. Rehearse your presentation. Use the language in Activity 4.

6 Give your presentation to the class. What important things did you learn from your classmates' information?

7 Think Fast! As a class, list all the majors mentioned in your presentations! (45 secs)

Culture

1 What do you know about Norway? Complete the fact file with information from the box. Then search online to check your answers.

> Oslo   5,214,900   69,712   13.1

Norway: The Best Country in the World for Young People!

According to a ranking released in 2015, the Scandinavian country offers the most attractive living conditions for people who are 15–24 years old.

In 2015, the non-governmental organization Youthonomics published the first edition of its Global Index, which ranked 64 countries according to different criteria, such as early education, higher education, access to employment and health care, among others. Norway was on the top of the ranking. But why was this country, with a population around 5 million inhabitants, the winner? See the main reasons below:

- Higher education and **vocational training**: young Norwegians have wide access to high-quality college education and training in skills that enable young people to enter the job market.

- Access to employment: levels of unemployment among young people are low and the country offers a positive environment for young **entrepreneurs**.

- Work and living conditions: besides having good salaries, young people in Norway are not discriminated against in the workplace.

- Well-being: young Norwegians feel safe and integrated into society, and their **civil rights** are fully respected.

Norway Fact File	
Capital city:	_____
Population:	_____ people (2015)
Percentage of the population 15–24 years old:	_____ %
GDP (per capita / year)	$_____
Interesting fact:	In the summer, days last around 20 hours. In the winter, however, there are only _____ hours of sunlight per day!

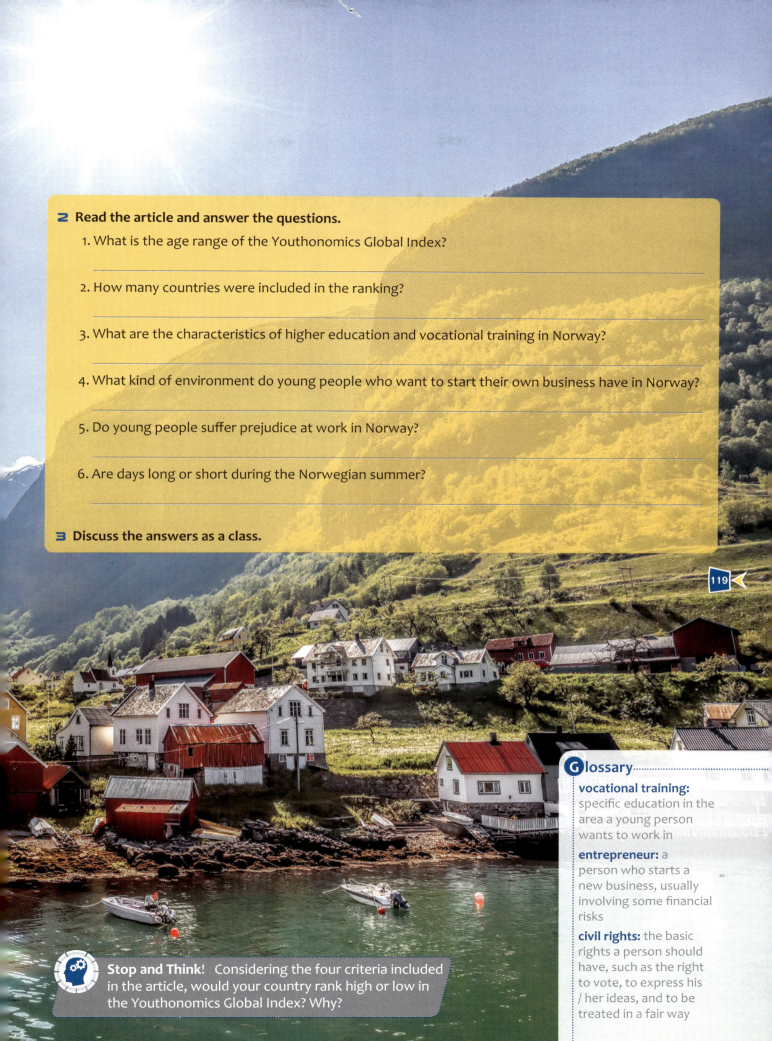

2 Read the article and answer the questions.

1. What is the age range of the Youthonomics Global Index?

2. How many countries were included in the ranking?

3. What are the characteristics of higher education and vocational training in Norway?

4. What kind of environment do young people who want to start their own business have in Norway?

5. Do young people suffer prejudice at work in Norway?

6. Are days long or short during the Norwegian summer?

3 Discuss the answers as a class.

Stop and Think! Considering the four criteria included in the article, would your country rank high or low in the Youthonomics Global Index? Why?

Glossary

vocational training: specific education in the area a young person wants to work in

entrepreneur: a person who starts a new business, usually involving some financial risks

civil rights: the basic rights a person should have, such as the right to vote, to express his / her ideas, and to be treated in a fair way

Project

1 Read the action plan for Connor's future academic life. Choose a heading from the box for each column.

Action   Deadline   Problem and Possible Solution   Resources (People / Things)   Tasks

Action Plan – Academic Life

Date: Sept 2   Name: Connor Nowak   Main goal: Becoming a doctor

① Get info about pre-med undergraduate programs.	- Talk to Ms. Brown (school counselor) about the best pre-med programs in the country. - Do some research online about Ms. Brown's recommendations.	- This week - Until the end of the month	- Ms. Brown - Notebook	- Ms. Brown will go on maternity leave soon – talk to her this week! - It might be difficult to find reliable info. - Talk to students who are in the programs.
② Get info about the medical career.	- Call Dr. Taylor to try to make an appointment with her (ask her about her job at her practice). - Get in touch with residents at General Hospital (talk to them about how they see their career).	- Mid-Oct - End of Oct	- Dr. Taylor (get Mom to talk to her?) - Friendly residents ☺	- Residents might not have time, or be willing to talk to me – try to get their email and introduce myself first.

Guess What!
In the United States, people who want to become doctors can't enroll in medical school right after high school. They need to get a bachelor's degree in a four-year "pre-med" program, usually in majors such as chemistry, biology or physics. After that, they can apply for a medical school.

120

2 Work in small groups. Read the action plan again and discuss the questions below.

1. Why is there a column for tasks in Connor's plan?
2. Do you think the possible problems Connor raised make sense? Why (not)?
3. Are the solutions he proposed to the problems efficient? Why (not)?
4. Would you add another column to Connor's action plan? If so, why?

3 Write an action plan for something you want to achieve in your life. Follow the steps below.

STEP 1
Think of an important thing you want to do in the future which demands planning and decision-making. Here are some suggestions:
- Taking a gap year
- Going to college / university
- Buying a car
- Getting a job
- Other: _____

STEP 2
Use a word processor (or a sheet of paper) to reproduce the chart on p. 120. Include your information and your main goal.

STEP 3
List all the actions you need to take to reach your objective.

STEP 4
Now write the tasks involved in each action—try to be as detailed as possible here.

STEP 5
Think of the deadlines carefully. They must be realistic and doable.

STEP 6
Consider all the resources—people and things—involved in each task.

STEP 7
Write all the possible problems you might face in each task. Also, think of ways of dealing with them.

STEP 8
When you have finished, review your plan. You might have to change the order of the actions or include new tasks.

4 Work in small groups. Share your action plan with your classmates.

Stop and Think! Do you think your action plan will help you reach your objective? If so, why?

Review

1 Underline the correct word to complete the collocations.

1. **be** / buy more patient with others
2. buy / **save** a car
3. travel / **get** a job
4. **get** / rent married
5. **have** / save a less stressful routine
6. travel / **rent** an apartment
7. buy / **save** money to buy a house
8. take / **save** resources, like water
9. **be** / start doing physical activities
10. **take** / travel a gap year
11. **travel** / take around the world

2 Use collocations from Activity 1 to label the pictures.

3 Are the sentences right (✓) or wrong (✗)? Look at the underlined information and rewrite the incorrect ones.

1. I yell at my brother very often. My mom keeps saying I need to <u>save resources</u>.
_____

2. I don't want to rent an apartment. How much money do I have to save to <u>buy a house</u>?
_____

3. Hailey has decided to take a gap year. She'll travel and do volunteer work <u>before going to college</u>.
_____

4. I want to <u>buy a car</u> instead of living on campus.
_____

4 Unscramble the sentences.

1. Lucy / will / after the holiday / working / be / ?
   _____

2. will / studying / on Thursday afternoon / be / you / English / ?
   _____

3. will / Mike and Dave / traveling / be / this summer / to the United States / ?
   _____

4. Fred Dawson / training / to be a doctor / will / at this time next year / be / ?
   _____

5 Match the questions in Activity 4 to the pictures. Then answer.

6 Complete the sentences with the correct form of the future continuous.

1. This time next year, I _____ (learn) French in France.
2. Dan and Mia _____ (get) married at this time tomorrow!
3. _____ Megan _____ (study) here next semester?
4. I can't talk to you between 5 and 6 p.m. I _____ (take) care of my little sister.
5. I'm so excited! In one week from now, Carrie and I _____ (live) in our own apartment!
6. What _____ you _____ (do) at this time tomorrow?

7 Answer the questions. Share your answers with a partner.

1. What will you be doing at this time tomorrow? _____
2. What will you be doing at 5 p.m. this Saturday? _____
3. What will you be doing next summer? _____
4. What will you be doing this time next year? _____

Just for Fun

1 Find the words in the mirrored word search to complete Michelle's plans.

My plans for the next decade:
1. Have a healthier _____
2. Be more _____
3. Go to _____ school
4. Start my own _____
5. Rent an _____ to live by myself
6. Travel around the _____
7. Save _____ to buy a house
8. Find Mr. Right and get _____

```
R E T N E M T R A P A V T K X
V C S K S V P Z P K R H G N V
U R A U J S L N M Y E N O M X
A M C T X V E D T W V T Z F D
D E I R R A M N M W N Q G V L
W P B I N T N E I T A P T N R
Z U G K P E L Y T S E F I L O
O W K C L N H B A A U B Q D W
V L A N O I T A C O V B X E U
M I L E S C S E N E W X K A E
```

2 Nick has a very ambitious future plan. Solve the puzzle to find it out!

Nick will be ___ ___ ___ ___ ___ ___ in ___ ___ ___ ___ ___ by this time next year!

1. The last letter in "travel."
2. The ninth letter of the alphabet.
3. The third letter in "save."
4. The second vowel in "business."
5. The letter that comes after "m."
6. A letter that the words "go" and "get" have in common.
7. This letter is in "cat," but not in "hat."
8. The eighth letter of the alphabet.
9. This letter is also a subject pronoun.
10. The sixth letter in "routine."
11. This letter is also an article.

Workbook

Unit 1

Vocabulary – Personality Traits

1 Find six positive personality traits in the word search.

F	B	I	X	D	C	A	Y	V	N	Z	X	X
R	H	E	T	A	R	E	D	I	S	N	O	C
I	I	R	Y	P	P	W	T	Z	E	V	T	P
E	H	B	G	V	Y	I	H	Q	W	D	B	A
N	S	X	F	B	L	G	O	E	L	C	P	T
D	H	R	E	A	S	O	N	A	B	L	E	I
L	J	M	R	T	A	S	E	U	H	R	E	E
Y	F	Z	X	S	L	O	S	Z	I	J	S	N
I	Q	A	D	G	J	C	T	O	W	Z	X	T
G	F	E	L	B	I	S	N	O	P	S	E	R

0. _____friendly_____
1. _____
2. _____
3. _____
4. _____
5. _____

2 Complete the chart with the negative forms of the adjectives in Activity 1.

im-, ir-, in-	un-	dis-
impatient		

126

3 Complete each sentence with a word in the box.

> friendly   honest   ~~inconsiderate~~   irresponsible   patient   unreasonable

0. Daniel is so ___inconsiderate___ ! I told him that I was sad because my dog died, but he kept telling jokes and laughing.

1. Emily is a very _____ girl. Yesterday she found an envelope with $200, but instead of keeping the money, she gave it to a police officer.

2. I think Noah is kind of _____. He's always late for class and rarely does his homework.

3. Dylan plays a lot with his siblings and helps them with their homework. He's a very _____ guy.

4. It's simply impossible to talk with Aileen when she's angry. She gets pretty _____ and loses her temper easily.

5. I believe Chloe will get the part-time job at the clothing store. She's really _____, and that's an important skill for a salesperson.

Guess What!
We use **so**, **very**, **pretty** and **really** to intensify an adjective, either positive or negative.

We use **kind of** to soften a negative adjective.

4 **Circle the correct word to complete the quotes.**

0. "No legacy is so rich as honest / (honesty)."

    William Shakespeare, English poet and playwright (1564-1616)

1. "You are not only responsible / responsibility for what you say, but also for what you do not say."

    Martin Luther, German religious leader (1483-1546)

2. "Have patient / patience. All things are difficult before they become easy."

    Saadi, Iranian poet (1184-1283)

3. "Nature is the mother and the habitat of man, even if sometimes a stepmother and an unfriendly / unfriendliness home."

    John Dewey, American philosopher (1859-1952)

4. "Perseverant / Perseverance is failing nineteen times and succeeding the twentieth."

    Julie Andrews, English actress (1935)

Grammar – Tag Questions

1 **Complete the sentences with a tag in the box.**

aren't we   didn't they   ~~don't you~~   did it   isn't she   will he

0. You like animals, _____don't you_____?
1. Olivia is a very friendly girl, _____?
2. Our school didn't won the competition, _____?
3. Tyler and Connor worked as volunteers last year, _____?
4. Mr. Carson won't be our math teacher in senior year, _____?
5. Lauren and I are still friends, _____?

2 **Correct the mistakes in the tag questions.**

STEVEN: Hi, welcome to Happy Paws, Kaitlyn. I like your resume! You work with kids, **didn't you**?   0. _____don't you_____

KAITLYN: Yes, I do. I love children… and animals.

STEVEN: And you worked at SeaLife. That aquarium closed down, **didn't they**?   1. _____

KAITLYN: Yes, unfortunately. But that is not a problem for my application, **are they**?   2. _____

STEVEN: Of course not! Let's see… you can work three hours a week, **can you**?   3. _____

KAITLYN: Yes, I can. But I can't work on Sundays.

Unit 1

3 Complete each sentence with a tag question. Then match the sentences to the pictures.

0. We can't park our car here, ____can we____?
1. Nick is really hungry, _____?
2. Sophia's English test was difficult, _____?
3. Your young sister is learning to ride a bike, _____?
4. Doug won't arrive in time for his job interview, _____?
5. They really like their cat, _____?

Review

1 Complete the chart.

Personality Trait	Person I Know	Why?
0. friendly	My cousin Emma	She is always smiling and has a nice word to say to everyone.
1. considerate		
2. impatient		
3. honest		
4. unreasonable		
5. responsible		

Reading

1 Read the text and complete it with the headings of three of the tips.

a. Dress for success
b. Learn about the position
c. Answer the questions

Five Tips to Ace Your Volunteer Work Interview

Applying for a volunteer position? Read our tips to help you have a successful interview.
Tip #1: Learn about the organization. Find as much information as possible about the institution you want to volunteer for. The interviewer won't test you on this kind of information, but you can use your research to show you are really interested in the institution.
Tip #2: _____. If you don't know exactly what tasks the position involves, don't be afraid to ask the recruiter! But do it before the interview.
Tip #3: _____. Forget clothes that are too casual: the way you dress for an interview shows how seriously you are going to take the volunteer work. For teen boys, a nice pair of pants and a shirt will do, but if you really want to impress, add a tie to the outfit. Teen girls should not wear too much make up or jewelry.
Tip #4: Be on time. Being late for an interview is unacceptable. Carefully plan your journey to the place where the interview will happen. Will someone take you? Will you use public transportation? How is the traffic in the area?
Tip #5: _____. It's pretty easy to get sidetracked when answering questions. Or you might be too nervous and end up giving monosyllabic answers, or speaking too much. Take a deep breath to calm down and concentrate on the interviewer. He/she understands that you are nervous—he/she has been in your shoes!
If you need more advice, talk to your parents, older siblings or to your teacher! They will be more than happy to help you!

2 Read and rank the volunteers from 1 - 3 with 1 having the best chance to get the volunteer position at Happy Paws.

- Lukas arrived on time and dressed well. However, he thought he was applying for a fundraising position, when in fact Happy Paws was hiring a vet assistant. ☐
- Melissa didn't arrive on time—her bus got stuck in traffic and she apologized sincerely to the interviewer. She knew everything about Happy Paws and the position, and answered all the questions with confidence. ☐
- Jackson wore baggy pants, a T-shirt, sneakers and a hat. He didn't arrive on time and was so nervous that he could only give monosyllabic answers. ☐

Writing

3 Work with a partner. Complete a mind map in your notebook with your own ideas about one of the tips below. Then write about the tip.

Go on your own   Be polite   Be prepared to ask questions

Unit 2

Vocabulary – Practical Inventions

1 Complete the sentences using some of the words below.

> hammer   saw   plywood   nails   solder   soldering iron
> hot glue gun   glue stick   drill   screwdriver   screw

1. Pass me the _____ and _____. I want to hang up this picture.
2. Can I borrow your _____? I need to make holes in the wall before I can put up the shelves.
3. This project uses metal parts. You'll have to get a _____ to connect them.
4. I'm building a bookshelf. Should I attach the pieces with nails or _____?
5. Where is the _____? Do you need the Phillips head or flat?

2 Complete the mind maps with the materials and tools you would use in each case.

Picture

hammer   nails

a broken vase

bookshelves

Grammar – Verbs in Past Participle

3 Find and write the past participle of each verb to make a passive form.

0. see — seen
1. be — _____
2. invent — _____
3. make — _____
4. develop — _____
5. use — _____
6. announce — _____
7. show — _____
8. invite — _____
9. write — _____
10. take — _____

D	D	K	P	A	V	D	R	N	D
E	I	N	V	I	T	E	D	E	U
T	M	I	R	X	K	V	N	K	S
N	P	R	L	N	J	E	N	A	E
E	S	E	E	N	W	L	Z	T	D
V	D	E	C	N	U	O	N	N	A
N	B	Q	W	M	B	P	H	M	D
I	P	K	D	L	A	E	D	S	P
H	U	X	D	F	R	D	K	O	U
N	E	T	T	I	R	W	E	X	F

Active vs. Passive Voice

1 Label each sentence as *A* (Active) or *P* (Passive). Underline the active or passive verb.

0. The airplane was invented by Wilber and Orville Wright in 1903.   P
1. Wilber and Orville Wright invented the airplane in 1903.   _____
2. In 1976, Steve Jobs and Steve Wozniak created Apple Computer.   _____
3. In 1976, Apple Computer was created by Steve Jobs and Steve Wozniak.   _____
4. The city council is improving public transportation.   _____
5. Public transportation has been improved recently.   _____
6. More and more people are using Facebook.   _____
7. Facebook is being used by more and more people.   _____
8. A robot that does your homework is being developed!   _____
9. My neighbor is developing a robot that does your homework!   _____

Unit 2

2 Read the text and circle the correct option.

The city of Memphis, Tennessee in the United States (1) **is known / is knew** as the birthplace of Rock and Roll. It (2) **is locate / is located** in the southwest corner of Tennessee, on the Mississippi River. The city's most famous musician, Elvis Presley, (3) **was born / is born** in nearby Tupelo, Mississippi, but moved to Memphis with his family when he was in 8th grade. Elvis's music is considered the earliest form of Rock and Roll, but it (4) **was influenced / were influenced** a great deal by Gospel music. Memphis (5) **was founded / is founded** in 1819, making it a relatively newer city. Before it (6) **was incorporated / is incorporated** as a city, native people such as the Chickasaw had been living there for thousands of years. The city's location (7) **was chose / was chosen** for its bluff site near the Mississippi River. Today the Memphis Metropolitan area has a population of 1.3 million and is an attraction for tourists. The Memphis Pyramid (8) **was built / had built** in 1989 and (9) **used / was used** as a sports arena before being used as a hotel and sporting goods store. Today Memphis is a thriving metropolis and the second largest city in the state of Tennessee.

Review

1 Complete each sentence with the correct passive form. Then match.

0. A hammer __is used__ — a. by combining an inclined plane and a nail.
1. The soldering gun _____ (invent) — b. to hit a nail.
2. Saws _____ (call) — c. by many names: hand, circular and hack saw.
3. The hot glue gun _____ (develop) — d. for people to weld metal.
4. A drill _____ (use) — e. to make it faster to stick things together.
5. The screw _____ (made) — f. to make holes in wood or concrete.

Reading

1 Read the text and circle T (True) or F (False).

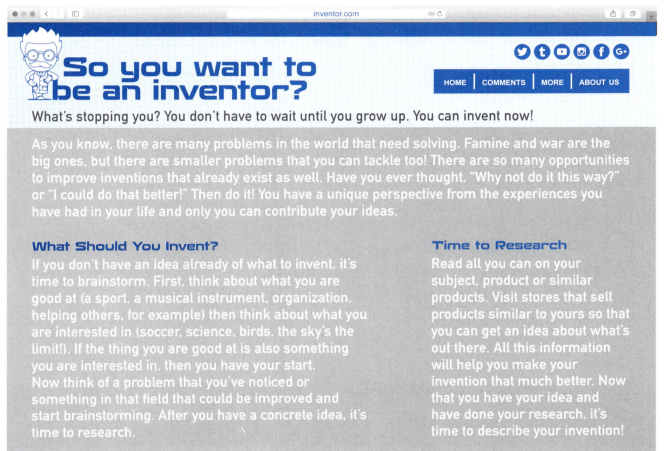

So you want to be an inventor?

What's stopping you? You don't have to wait until you grow up. You can invent now!

As you know, there are many problems in the world that need solving. Famine and war are the big ones, but there are smaller problems that you can tackle too! There are so many opportunities to improve inventions that already exist as well. Have you ever thought, "Why not do it this way?" or "I could do that better!" Then do it! You have a unique perspective from the experiences you have had in your life and only you can contribute your ideas.

What Should You Invent?
If you don't have an idea already of what to invent, it's time to brainstorm. First, think about what you are good at (a sport, a musical instrument, organization, helping others, for example) then think about what you are interested in (soccer, science, birds, the sky's the limit!). If the thing you are good at is also something you are interested in, then you have your start. Now think of a problem that you've noticed or something in that field that could be improved and start brainstorming. After you have a concrete idea, it's time to research.

Time to Research
Read all you can on your subject, product or similar products. Visit stores that sell products similar to yours so that you can get an idea about what's out there. All this information will help you make your invention that much better. Now that you have your idea and have done your research, it's time to describe your invention!

1. You have to be 18 to invent. — T F
2. Brainstorming is a good way to think up something to invent. — T F
3. An invention can be coming up with something new or improving something that already exists. — T F
4. It's not necessary to do research when you are inventing your product. — T F
5. You should invent because your unique perspective is valuable. — T F

Writing

2 Think of an invention and write a paragraph about it in your notebook. Be sure to write about:

- The problem: What did you notice that needed a solution or improvement? Describe it. Example: A soccer ball that doesn't go flat.
- Your skills and experience: What allowed you to be able to identify the problem and what makes you able to solve it? Example: I play soccer all the time and I get so tired of the ball going flat.
- A list of all the things you will need to create it. Example: five soccer balls, five types of glue, a pump, etc.
- The process of inventing it. How will you invent your product? What experiments or trials will you do? Example: I'll buy five kinds of glue and apply them to the soccer ball and test if any of them keep the ball from going flat.

3 Unit

Vocabulary – Activities

1 Read the prompts and write the name of the activity. Use the words in the box.

> learn a foreign language   write a book   start a band with your friends
> get a part-time job   travel abroad alone   create a vlog

0. audience / microphone / musicians — *Start a band with your friends.*
1. suitcase / passport / money _____
2. work after school / responsibility _____
3. video camera / ideas to share _____
4. podcasts / flashcards / dictionary _____
5. computer or paper and pen _____

2 Match the parts of the sentence. Then number the pictures each sentence refers to.

0. I'm a talented musician, so
1. I want to earn my own money, so
2. I've always wanted to perform, so
3. I'm great with mechanical things, so
4. I'm creative and I love computers, so
5. I want to travel to Europe, so

a. I'm learning a foreign language.
b. I'm going to start a band with my friends.
c. I want to build a drone.
d. I want to develop my own computer game.
e. I think I'll attend acting classes this year.
f. I'm going to get a part-time job.

3 Write the activities you would recommend for each person. Use the words from Activity 1.

0

Tom likes singing and is a great guitar player.
Start a band with friends.

1

Carla is very outgoing and likes an audience.
_____

2

Erick has always loved playing games and is creative.
_____

3

Jose and Omar love taking things apart and putting them back together.
_____

4

Vivian is very responsible and disciplined and has always wanted to earn money.
_____

5

Dana wants to see the world and loves adventure.
_____

Grammar – Present Perfect

Present Perfect and Present Perfect Continuous

1 Read and label the actions as finished or still in progress.

0. I have been playing the violin since I was a child.   ___ finished   _X_ still in progress
1. My family has been to the US.   ___ finished   ___ still in progress
2. Have you ever eaten Indian food?   ___ finished   ___ still in progress
3. My teacher has been developing a drone.   ___ finished   ___ still in progress
4. How long have you been writing your book?   ___ finished   ___ still in progress
5. Kylie has traveled abroad alone before.   ___ finished   ___ still in progress

Unit 3

Present Perfect Continuous

2 Complete the sentences using the present perfect continuous.

0. My aunt ____has been studying____ (study) Arabic for two years.
1. Kevin _____ (build) a drone out of recycled parts.
2. Since it's been raining so much we _____ (practice – neg) soccer lately.
3. My sister is so creative. She _____ (develop) a racing video game.
4. I've had **writer's block** this week, so I _____ (write – neg) my novel.

Present Perfect Simple vs. Present Perfect Continuous

3 Read and circle the correct verbs.

0. My brother **has attended** / **(has been attending)** acting classes since last year. He loves them!
1. Kim **has traveled abroad** / **has been traveling abroad** alone. I can't believe her parents let her go!
2. Dan **has built** / **has been building** a drone. He's proud of his accomplishment.
3. Did you know Kelly **has been writing** / **has written** a book? It was published last year.
4. My cousin **has developed** / **has been developing** a computer game. It's not finished yet.

4 Complete the sentences using *since* or *for*.

0. My brother and I have been studying German ____since____ we were in kindergarten.
1. My best friend Jan has been vlogging _____ two years.
2. Our teacher has been traveling to Poland every summer _____ a decade.
3. Mr. Williamson has been working as a lawyer _____ 2014.
4. I've been writing a book _____ about six months.

Review

1 Complete the sentences using the present perfect continuous or the present perfect.

DIANA: All of these school clubs look so fun! I can't decide which one to choose.

SARAH: I know! They do! You know, I have always wanted to try acting!

DIANA: I (0) ____have been attending____ (attend) acting classes since last year. It's a blast!

SARAH: What about the writing club? I (1) _____ (write) a book before. It was about a teen band.

DIANA: That could be fun, but what about the foreign language club?
I (2) _____ (learn) Italian this semester and I'm pretty good at it!

SARAH: I prefer more creative activities. I might join the vloggers club.
I (3) _____ (create – neg) a vlog but it looks like so much fun.

DIANA: Well, the great thing is that there are so many opportunities to choose from.
I (4) _____ (have – neg) such a hard time making a decision before!

Glossary

writer's block: when an author can't think of what to write about

> 136

Reading

1 Read and correct the false statements below.

The Benefits And Drawbacks Of Teens Getting Part-Time Jobs

Adolescence is a transition period. Teens want to become more independent from their parents and be able to make their own decisions. One way they can do that is by getting a part-time job, but of course a teen and their parents need to consider the benefits and drawbacks. Here are just a few.

Benefits of getting a part-time job:

- Working for their own money gives teens a sense of responsibility. They can contribute to the household or their own expenses.
- Teens can learn how to manage money effectively, which is an important skill for their future.
- Working part-time as a teenager provides valuable work experience which can be included on a resume.
- Having a part-time job keeps teens busy and out of trouble.
- Teens can form good work habits including time management.

Drawbacks of getting a part time job:

- Teens who work have less time for homework, which can lead to lower grades.
- Working teens also have less time for recreational activities such as sports, which can promote healthy, balanced living.
- Balancing work and school can lead to increased stress.
- Teens may misspend their money before they've developed responsibility.

Of course whether a part-time job is right or not depends on the particular teenager and his or her situation. The teenager and his or her parents should sit down and discuss these pros and cons as well as the teen's personality and track record of responsibility before making this important decision.

0. One benefit of a part-time job for a teenager is having increased stress.

   One drawback of a part-time job for a teenager is having increased stress.

1. Having a part-time job can keep teens out of trouble.

2. Teens who work have less time for homework.

3. The money a teen earns from a part-time job should be for his or her own use. Teens can't contribute to household expenses.

4. Deciding whether a teen should work a part-time job depends only on the benefits and drawbacks mentioned in the article.

Writing

2 In your notebook, write about a part-time job you want to have. Include:

- A description of the job (Where is it?, What responsibilities do you have?, Who are your coworkers?)
- Your skills and qualifications (What experiences have you had in the past that qualify you? What have you been doing recently that's relevant to your job responsibilities?)

Unit 4

Vocabulary – Sustainable Living

1 Complete the sentences using the words below.

> baking soda   car pool   white vinegar   indoor garden   electric bike
> rechargeable batteries   reusable shopping bags   food leftovers

0. Using ____rechargeable batteries____ not only reduces waste, it reduces contamination of the land when they decompose and release dangerous chemicals.

1. Did you know that shipping food from one place to another uses resources like gasoline and packaging material? Having an _____ eliminates this.

2. One great way to save gas and reduce air pollution in your city is to organize a _____ with a neighbor if you are going to the same school or workplace.

3. Did you know that common household cleaning chemicals can be dangerous for the environment and your health? Use _____ and _____ instead.

4. Want to reduce your use of plastic? One important way is to bring your own _____ to the grocery store.

5. If you want to reduce the air pollution in your city, you can take public transportation or an _____.

6. It's a good idea to use _____ to make a second meal. That way you don't waste food and if you eat it soon, it still has lots of vitamins and minerals.

2 Which sentence from Activity 1 do these pictures refer to? Number them.

3 Cross out the word that doesn't belong. Explain why it's different.

0. reusable shopping bags / ~~white vinegar~~ / rechargeable batteries
   Both reusable shopping bags and rechargeable batteries reduce waste.

1. car pool / electric bike / baking soda
   _____

2. indoor garden / white vinegar / baking soda
   _____

3. reusable shopping bags / indoor garden / food leftovers
   _____

4 **Match the sentences.**

0. What can I use for a good natural scrub cleanser?
1. My parents won't let me order a pizza.
2. I hate using plastic bags.
3. I don't have a yard to plant vegetables.
4. It's important to recycle batteries.
5. How can I use vinegar to clean?
6. Why don't we ride to school together?
7. I get tired riding my bike all the way to school.

a. Really? I just use rechargeable ones.
b. Get some reusable ones!
c. How about baking soda?
d. Great! Let's organize a carpool with our friends.
e. You don't need one for an indoor garden.
f. It's because you have leftovers in the fridge.
g. It's great for windows and surfaces.
h. Why don't you use an electric one?

Grammar – First vs. Second Conditional

1 **Read and circle the correct verb.**

0. If you ride your bike or take the bus, you (will) / would save gas and reduce air pollution.
1. If everyone in the city rode a bike or took the bus, it will / would save gas and reduce air pollution tremendously!
2. If all of Brazil banned plastic bags, it will / would cut down on trash in the streets.
3. If chemical companies only produced baking soda and vinegar-based cleaning products, it will / would reduce the use of harmful chemicals a great deal.
4. If your family starts using baking soda and vinegar for cleaning, it will / would reduce the use of harmful chemicals in your house.
5. If plastic garbage weren't thrown into the ocean, we will / would save thousands of sea animals per year.
6. If we recycle a single aluminium can, we will / would save enough electricity to power a TV for a couple of hours.
7. If we continue polluting the environment, millions of animal species will / would face extinction.
8. If you took your electronic devices to a recycling center, you will / would prevent many people from developing diseases like cancer.

 Unit

2 **Complete the sentences.**

0. If my little brother stops taking his medicine, he ____will____ get sick.
1. If I don't study for my exam, I _____ fail.
2. If our city only allowed electric or hybrid cars on the roads, we _____ reduce air pollution a lot!
3. If my dad says I can go, I _____ see you at the party.
4. If politicians were serious about combating global climate change, we _____ all be using solar energy to power our homes.
5. If my family goes on vacation this summer, we _____ go to Cancun, Mexico!

3 **Complete the sentences by writing the result clause.**

0. If I won the lottery, <u>I would buy a house</u>.
1. If you do your homework, _____.
2. If we reduce our waste, _____.
3. If my dad stopped smoking, _____.
4. If my best friend moved away, _____.
5. If Daniel goes to the movies, _____.

Review

1 **Write about five changes you plan to make to help the environment and the result of those changes. Use the first conditional.**

0. <u>If I ride my bike to school, my parents will save money on gas and air pollution will be reduced.</u>
1. _____
2. _____
3. _____
4. _____
5. _____

Reading

1 **Read the title. Mark (✓) the ideas you think the text will mention. Then read and check.**

a. ✓ The definition of climate change.
b. ___ More ways to go green.
c. ___ The importance of recycling.
d. ___ Energy efficiency.

The Problem of Climate Change and How You Can Help Solve It

The environment is in trouble. Many scientists and leaders call **climate change** the biggest problem facing our world today. You may have heard it called global warming, but the more accepted term is climate change because it doesn't only include warming, but other drastic changes in weather patterns such as hurricanes, floods and heat waves.

What causes climate change? Over the last fifty years, scientists began to notice an alarming increase in carbon dioxide in the atmosphere. An increase in this gas means that the heat of the Earth cannot escape the atmosphere easily. As a result, the heat is trapped inside the atmosphere and this leads to the temperature of the Earth increasing and all the extreme weather events that brings with it.

What can be done? Everyone on the planet has to decrease the amount of carbon dioxide that is released into the environment. In order to do that, we have to identify what releases it. The short answer is the burning of **fossil fuels**. Think about all the sources of energy you use, like the electricity that lights your house, the gas burned for cooking on your stove, etc. Even though when you turn on a light you can't see the coal or gas burning, it is, at the power plant, and then it's transferred to your house in the form of electricity. If your family has a car, it uses petroleum to run and the **exhaust** it releases adds to the carbon dioxide in the atmosphere.

How can I help? You know the main ways to go green: get reusable shopping bags, use rechargeable batteries and eat your leftovers! But you can also…

- Use energy-efficient light bulbs. The spiral bulbs last as much as five times longer than regular bulbs, but LED bulbs can last 10 years or more! They use less energy to provide the same light as well. Tell your parents to switch to LED.

- Eat less meat. Lots of people around the world are choosing to eat less meat. Not only is it better for your health, it reduces the enormous cost of producing meat. Did you know that it takes almost 2,000 gallons of water to produce a pound of beef? A great deal of resources are also used to raise the cow such as land and food, as well as energy to process the meat and the gas needed for the trucks that ship it. Go veggie, go green!

Glossary

climate change: a change in climate patterns, caused largely by increased levels of carbon dioxide in the atmosphere.

fossil fuel: a natural fuel such as coal or gas, formed in the geological past from the remains of living organisms.

exhaust: waste gases or air expelled from an engine, turbine or other machine in the course of its operation.

Writing

2 **In your notebook, fill in a chart with challenges to going green and solutions.**

Challenges	Solutions
There are no recycling bins at my school.	Start a petition asking the director to install them.

Vocabulary – Supernatural Things, Creatures and Phenomena

1 Label the pictures.

- zombies
- UFO
- telekinesis
- alien
- ghost
- werewolf

UFO

_____

_____

_____

_____

_____

2 Read and match the word with its definition.

alien	The supernatural power of seeing objects or action removed in space or time from natural viewing.
werewolf	Communication between minds by some means other than sensory perception.
clairvoyance	Any unexplained moving object observed in the sky, especially one assumed to be of extraterrestrial origin.
telekinesis	A human being who has changed into a wolf, while retaining human intelligence.
UFO	The supposed ability to move or deform inanimate objects, as metal spoons, through mental processes.
zombie	A creature from outer space, extraterrestrial.
telepathy	The body of a dead person given the semblance of life, but mute and will-less, by a supernatural force, usually for some evil purpose.
ghost	The soul of a dead person, a disembodied spirit imagined, usually as a vague, shadowy form, as wandering among or haunting living persons.

3 Read and correct the mistake in each sentence. Pay attention to the words in bold.

0. I dressed up as a **zombie** for Halloween. It was such a simple costume, just a sheet with two holes for my eyes. _____ghost_____

1. My little brother swears that he saw a **werewolf** flying over our house. It was green and lit up the sky. _____

2. Mrs. Stenson says that she has the gift of **telekinesis**. She can communicate with others by reading their minds. _____

3. I believe in **zombies**. The universe is so huge that I think it's likely there is life on other planets. _____

Grammar – Modals of Speculation

1 Read and match the facts with the speculations.

(0) *Alien* is a 1979 British-American science fiction horror film. (1) It tells the story of an alien that stalks and kills the crew of a spaceship. (2) The film was highly acclaimed and won an Academy Award for Best Visual Effects. (3) *Alien* has inspired novels, comic books, video games and toys based on the film. (4) The movie had three sequels.

- ☐ They might have spent a lot of money on the graphics.
- [0] It must have been written and produced in English.
- ☐ It could have entered through the escape hatch.
- ☐ They might not have made as much money as the original.
- ☐ It couldn't have been more popular than E.T.!

2 Look at the pictures and circle the word to complete the sentence.

He **(must have)** / **may have** been surprised. He **(might have)** / **couldn't have** hurt his back.

He **could have** / **must have been** killed! He **must not have** / **might have** been careful.

He **might not have** / **must not have** seen the banana peel on the floor. He **could have** / **might not have** broken his leg.

3 Read and choose the correct meaning of the response.

0. A: Who ate the last cookie?
   B: It can't have been Brad. He's on a diet.
   <u>I'm sure it wasn't Brad.</u> / Maybe it was Brad.

1. A: I can't find my wallet.
   B: You must have left it in the car.
   I think you left it in the car. / *I'm sure you left it in the car.*

2. A: Did you see Jim at work?
   B: He works in a different department. He might have been there.
   I'm not sure if he was there. / *I'm certain he was there.*

3. A: I don't believe he won the race.
   B: He won? He couldn't have won!
   I don't believe he won either. / *It's possible that he won.*

4. A: Why are the police outside your neighbor's house?
   B: I don't know. There could have been an accident.
   I'm sure there was an accident. / *It's possible that there was an accident.*

Unit 5

4 Read and rewrite the underlined sentences using modal verbs and keeping the same meaning.

0. I saw a bright light in the sky. <u>I'm certain it was a UFO.</u>
   <u>It must have been a UFO.</u>

1. My cousin told me he is telepathic. <u>Maybe he didn't tell the truth.</u>
   ___

2. I had a dream an alien visited me from outer space but she left right away. <u>I don't think she wanted to hurt me.</u>
   ___

3. A ghost visited Kimmy last week and called her by her nickname. <u>She says it had to be her great grandmother.</u>
   ___

4. Mr. Byrd lost all his money in the lottery. <u>He's definitely wasn't clairvoyant!</u>
   ___

Review

1 Write a sentence speculating about what may have happened in each photo. Use a past modal and the appropriate vocabulary word.

0. <u>The zombies must have come back to life.</u>

1. ___

2. ___

3. ___

Reading

1 Read the article. Then complete each definition with an underlined word from the article.

0. _____mainstream_____ : principal, dominant, or widely accepted.
1. _____ : a person with an exceptional intellect.
2. _____ : to repeat words, as from memory.

Pg. 33   THE DAILY NEWS   July

5-Year-Old Genius Boy Allegedly Telepathic

Ramses Sanguino is a five-year-old boy from Los Angeles, California. He suffers from autism, a developmental disorder of children that often impairs communication. He is also considered a <u>genius</u>, already learning seven languages and able to solve algebra problems.

The skill that attracted the attention of neuroscientists, however, is his ability to recount numbers that have not been show to him. His mother writes down a series of numbers, up to 38, out of his sight and the boy has been shown to be able to <u>recite</u> them. He can also recount the value and suits of playing cards that are hidden from his view.

Dr. Diane Powell, a neuroscientist in Oregon, U.S., saw the boy's skill through the videos his mother posted online and invited him for a study. Her research focuses on the alternative methods of communication that children with autism use and believes that telepathy may be one of them. It makes sense, she believes, that children who have difficulty communicating in their native language, may be better able to communicate in other ways.

Dr. Powell has been researching telepathy and has met seven other people who show signs of the ability. She recognizes that <u>mainstream</u> scientists do not accept that telepathy is real, but she says she has seen evidence of it and is driven to study the phenomenon despite what others say.

Ramses' mother's main concern is that her son gets the best education possible. She put him in a normal preschool, but he was so much more advanced than the other children that she decided to take him out and is looking for a special school for him. "I really hope one day that Ramses will invent a cure for cancer or something great like that," says his mom. "He is so smart that sometimes he scares me."

---

2 Read and find...

0. Ramses' age: _____5 years old_____
1. One of Ramses' skills: _____
2. Mainstream scientist's view on telepathy: _____
3. Why Dr. Powell thinks children with autism may be more likely to be telepathic:
   _____
   _____

Writing

3 Answer the following questions in your notebook. Then share your answers with the class.
- Which of the following phenomena do you think is the most likely to be real?
  telepathy   telekinesis   clairvoyance
- Or if you don't think any are possible, explain why.
- Have you known anyone or known of anyone with one of these gifts?
- What could they do?
- How did you know it was real?

Unit 6

Vocabulary – Milestones of the 20th Century

1 Read and match.

0. economic — c
1. World
2. Russian
3. flu
4. nuclear
5. Cuban missile

a. War
b. disaster
c. crisis (2x)
d. pandemic
e. Revolution

2 Read and circle the correct verb.

0. Scientist Marie Curie had / **made** an important discovery. She discovered radium.
1. Fidel Castro and Che Guevara **led** / made the Cuban revolution in 1953.
2. The Mexican government distributed masks to **resist** / **fight** the swine flu in 2009.
3. When the 2008 global economic crisis **hit** / **appeared**, many countries were affected.
4. In 2015, traces of liquid water were found on Mars. Scientists who discovered this **achieved** / **won** a major scientific breakthrough.

Che Guevara

3 Match the sentence halves.

0. In 1952, Jonas Salk achieved…
1. In Fukushima, Japan in 2011 a nuclear…
2. Because there were few resources to fight…
3. The Second World…
4. The Great Depression in 1929 was one of the worst economic…

a. the pandemic, 50 million people died in the Bubonic Plague in the Late Middle Ages.
b. crises the world had seen.
c. a major breakthrough with the discovery of a polio vaccine.
d. War was one of the deadliest in modern history.
e. disaster occurred following a major earthquake.

146

Guess What!
The Mexican Revolution began in 1910 and 1.5 million people died. The war lasted over a decade and radically transformed Mexican culture and government.

4 **Complete the quotes using a word below.**

~~war~~ ~~breakthroughs~~ revolution discovery economic

"Industrial opportunities are going to stem more from the biological sciences than from chemistry and physics. I see biology as being the greatest area of scientific ___breakthroughs___ in the next generation."
— George E. Brown, Jr.

"History reminds us that dictators and despots arise during times of severe _____ crisis."
— Robert Kiyosaki

"Writing is a journey of _____ because until you start, you never know what will happen, and you can be surprised by what you do—expect the unexpected!"
— Mini Grey

"To be prepared for _____ is one of the most effective means of preserving peace."
— George Washington

"Those who make peaceful _____ impossible will make violent revolution inevitable."
— John F. Kennedy

Grammar – Third and Mixed Conditionals

1 **Read and mark (✓) the correct verb.**

0. If the levies in New Orleans had not been breached, Hurricane Katrina _____ so many lives.
   - [✓] would not have taken
   - [ ] would not take

1. If the negotiations regarding the Cuban Missile Crisis had not been successful, there _____ a full-scale nuclear war.
   - [ ] might have been
   - [ ] might be

2. If scientists hadn't successfully cloned Dolly the sheep, there _____ so many other cloned animals today.
   - [ ] would not have been
   - [ ] would not be

3. If the United States had not started the Afghanistan and Iraq wars, over 50,000 Americans _____.
   - [ ] would not have been killed
   - [ ] would not be killed

4. If fires had not broken out as a result of the San Francisco Earthquake, so much of the city _____.
   - [ ] would not have been destroyed
   - [ ] would not be destroyed

2 **Complete the sentences using the correct form of the verb in parentheses.**

If I (0) ___had not gotten___ (not-get) a flu vaccine, I (1) _____ (have) the flu this year. If my sister and I (2) _____ (not-practice) the guitar, we (3) _____ (not-be) so good at it now.

If the U.S. (4) _____ (not-join) the Vietnam War, there (5) _____ (not-be) so many lives lost.

3 Complete the sentences with your own ideas.

1. If I had been born in another country, _____
2. If my mother had been famous, _____
3. If I had been born blind, _____
4. If my parents had been to Europe, _____
5. If I had gone to college at 13 years old, _____

4 Make sentences about what the world would be like if the following things hadn't been invented. Share your ideas with a partner.

0. the computer: *If the computer hadn't been invented, we would all read a lot more books and newspapers.*

1. the cell phone: _____

2. the airplane: _____

3. the automobile: _____

4. vaccines: _____

5. electricity: _____

Review

1 Are the sentences correct (C) or incorrect (I)? Correct the incorrect sentences.

0. If scientists hadn't achieved so many scientific breakthroughs, our quality of life today would be lower. __C__

1. If the Second World War had not broken out, many lives would be saved. _____

2. Influenza might have spread if the government hadn't given funds to fight the pandemic. _____

3. The U.S. might still be a colony of England, if the rebels had led the American Revolution. _____

4. If we hadn't moved to a hurricane zone, our house would not have flooded every year. _____

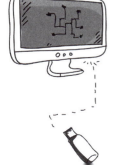

Reading

1 What do you know about the Fukushima nuclear disaster? Discuss the answers to the following questions with a partner. Then read and check your answers.

1. When and where did Fukushima occur?
2. What happened at Fukushima?
3. How bad was the nuclear disaster compared to other disasters in history?

The Fukushima Nuclear Disaster

On March 11, 2011, an earthquake with a magnitude of 9.0 hit off the northeastern coast of Japan. It was a rare, double quake which had a severe duration of three minutes. This quake was the most powerful to ever hit Japan and the fourth most powerful quake in the world. The quake caused the seafloor to shift, which caused a tsunami, or a giant wave, that flooded an area of 560 square kilometers. Nineteen thousand people died and over a million buildings were destroyed.

The Fukushima I Nuclear Power Plant was in operation at the time and the tsunami flooded the site. The **reactors** automatically shut down, but the emergency **generators** cooling the reactors were destroyed, causing the reactors to overheat, which led to the **nuclear meltdown** and the release of radioactive material into the area. It was the second largest nuclear disaster after Chernobyl.

One-hundred fifty-four thousand people living in the area were evacuated by the government and many people outside of the mandatory evacuation zone decided to leave for fear for their own safety. Many of these people are still **displaced** today because the area has still not been ruled safe for human habitation.

While no people died immediately from exposure to the radiation, local populations of birds and other animals have been reduced and the effects of exposure to radiation, which may include higher **incidence** of cancer, may continue into the future.

2 Mark each statement T (True) or F (False).

0. An earthquake caused a tsunami which led to the destruction of the nuclear power plant in Fukushima. (T) F
1. Nineteen thousand people died from the flooding and destruction caused by the tsunami. T F
2. The Fukushima nuclear disaster was worse than Chernobyl. T F
3. Everyone who was evacuated has returned to their homes. T F
4. There is a concern about increased cancer risk among those exposed to radiation. T F
5. If the flooding hadn't destroyed the generators, the release of radioactive material into the area wouldn't have happened. T F

Writing

3 Research about another famous nuclear disaster. In your notebook, write about:

- Where and when it happened
- What the consequences were
- What would have happened differently if the events had been different

Glossary

reactor: the device in which the nuclear-fission chain reaction occurs for generating radiation

generator: a machine that converts one form of energy into another

nuclear meltdown: the melting of the nuclear reactor core that could lead to the release of radiation

displaced: taken away from their homes

incidence: the rate of occurrence

Unit 7

Vocabulary – Living Abroad

1 Choose the verb to complete the sentences.

Thousands of students study abroad every year where they have new experiences and (0.) **get /(make)** new friends. There is a lot to do to prepare, such as (1.) **apply for / try** a student visa and (2.) **get / take out** a passport if you don't already have one. You need to (3.) **choose / get** a school, (4.) **take out / enroll in** a course and (5.) **make / fill out** forms. Then it's time to (6.) **buy / choose** plane tickets and (7.) **do / make** travel arrangements. Once you get to the foreign country, all that work is worth it! You will be able to (8.) **try / take out** new food and (9.) **make / participate in** local events. It will be the experience of a lifetime!

2 Complete the dialogue with the correct part of the collocation.

GINA: I'm so excited! I'm going to study abroad in Germany next semester.

JOEL: That's great! Did you (0.) _____get_____ your passport?

GINA: Yes, and now I have to (1.) _____ for my student visa.

JOEL: What about travel insurance?

GINA: I still need to (2.) _____ travel insurance and (3.) _____ plane tickets.

JOEL: Do you know what school you will (4.) _____?

GINA: No. I need to do that and (5.) _____ in a German course.

JOEL: I'm so jealous! You are going to (6.) _____ new friends and (7.) _____ local food.

GINA: Yes. I'm really looking forward to it. I want to (8.) _____ in local events too!

JOEL: There is a lot to do to get ready to study abroad, but the experience is so worth it!

GINA: For sure!

3 Choose the correct order of events to study abroad.

0. You have to _____choose a language school_____ before you can _____make new friends_____.
   a. choose a language school / make new friends
   b. make new friends / choose a language school

1. First you need to _____ before you _____.
   a. apply for a student visa / make travel arrangements
   b. make travel arrangements / apply for a student visa

2. It's necessary to _____ before you _____.
   a. choose a language school / enroll in a course
   b. enroll in a course / chose a language school.

3. You have to _____ before you can _____.
   a. try local food / fill out forms
   b. fill out forms / try local food.

4. You must _____ before you can _____.
   a. participate in local events / buy plane tickets
   b. buy plane tickets / participate in local events

Grammar – Reported Speech

1 Match the direct speech to the verb tense changes in reported speech.

0. simple past (*She tried local foods.*) — b. past perfect (*She had tried local foods.*)
1. present of be (*She tries local foods.*)
2. imperative (*Try local foods.*)
3. present continuous (*She's trying local foods.*)

a. past of be (*She tried local foods.*)
b. past perfect (*She had tried local foods.*)
c. past continuous (*She's trying local foods.*)
d. infinitive (*… to try local foods.*)

2 Mark (✓) the correct sentence in direct speech.

0. He said he was fishing in the ocean.

   ✓ "I'm fishing in the ocean."

   ___ "I was fishing in the ocean."

1. She asked if I had gone to the movies.

   ___ "Are you going to the movies?"

   ___ "Did you go to the movies?"

2. He asked if I went to the gym often.

   ___ "Do you go the gym often?"

   ___ "Are you going to the gym?"

3. May said she was applying for a student visa.

   ___ "I applied for a student visa."

   ___ "I'm applying for a student visa."

4. He asked me to close the door.

   ___ "Please, close the door."

   ___ "I'll close the door."

5. Rob said he had bought his plane ticket.

   ___ "I bought my plane ticket."

   ___ "I'm buying my plane ticket."

Unit 7

3 Read and circle the correct option in the sentence.

0. I said, "It's a great movie."
   I said it **was** / has been a great movie.

1. Jamie said, "Listen to her."
   He said **to listen** / listened to her.

2. Moni asked, "What are you doing?"
   She asked me what I **was doing** / did.

3. Luisa said, "I filled out the forms."
   She said she **had filled out** / filled out the forms.

4. Rick said, "I'm hungry."
   He said he **was** / be hungry.

5. Amanda asked, "Did you get your passport?"
   She asked if I **got** / had gotten my passport.

4 Look and rewrite the sentences in reported speech.

0. He said he had an exam tomorrow.
1. _____
2. _____
3. _____
4. _____
5. _____

Review

1 Complete the reported statement with the correct verb, changing the tense.

0. "I already took out travel insurance," said Jimena.
   Jimena said she _____had taken out_____ travel insurance.

1. Gladys said, "I'm making new friends."
   Gladys said she _____ new friends.

2. "Participate in local events," my mom told me.
   My mom told me _____ in local events.

3. "Choose a language school before you make travel arrangements," my teacher said.
   My teacher said _____ before I make travel arrangements.

4. "I enrolled in a Chinese course," said Danny.
   Danny said he _____ in a Chinese course.

Reading

1 Read the text and complete the headings of each body paragraph with the phrases below.

…makes you grow personally.   …helps you make life-long friends.
…opens your mind.   …gives you more career opportunities.
~~…allows you to learn another language.~~

Teen Traveler Blog: The Benefits of Studying Abroad

Today I want to talk to you about the benefits of studying abroad. As young people we are really, really lucky. Most of us don't have full time jobs that we have to keep. Most of us don't have children yet or aging parents we must care for. At this time in our lives we have a unique opportunity to study abroad and see the world. But what are the specific benefits?

Studying abroad <u>allows you to learn another language</u>

If you go to a country that doesn't speak your language, you will almost certainly learn the local language. Many colleges and universities have language classes for foreign students so that you can learn the language that your regular classes will be in while you are studying there. Living in another country for so long means that you will be interacting with local people and making friends. You will most likely be doing this in the local language, which will accelerate your learning of the language.

Studying abroad _____

Have you ever gone away from your hometown for a vacation and returned to see things around you differently? This means that you have experienced personal growth. All kinds of life experiences make us grow as people, but none so much as the **profound** experience of studying abroad. I guarantee that you will learn a lot about yourself. You'll develop more independence and self-confidence and you'll learn to see the world around you in a different way.

Studying abroad _____

Living in another country for a semester or a year teaches you things about life and about other cultures that you could never learn from books or TV. You learn another way of life deeply and it can change who you are and how you see the world. From food to festivals, from family relationships to work habits, living abroad shows you a different way to live.

Studying abroad _____

Companies want to hire employees with diverse experiences. (They also prefer bilingual employees!) If you can say that you have studied abroad in another country, it means you know the culture and the language and that gives you an advantage in almost any job field.

Studying abroad _____

You don't just meet friends when you study abroad, you create lasting friendships. This is because studying abroad will be such an incredible experience that it will **bind** you to the friends you make. You will learn about other cultures and world views and friendships with diverse people will continue to **enrich** your life as you maintain your connections with them.

2 Answer the questions in your notebook. Then discuss with a partner.

1. What is one way that studying abroad can help you in your career goals?
2. How does studying abroad open your mind?
3. Why does studying abroad allow you to make life-long friends?

Writing

3 In your notebook, write a reflection on what studying abroad would mean to you.

Consider the following points:
- Where would you like to study and why?
- What would you need to do to make study abroad possible for you?
- What benefits would studying abroad bring to you in particular?

Glossary

profound: entering deeply into subjects of thought or knowledge

bind: to tie together, to secure with a bond

enrich: to add greater value or significance to

Unit 8

Vocabulary – Arrangements and Plans

1 Complete the collocations. Then match them to the photos.

0. get — money
1. buy — an apartment
2. save — a healthier lifestyle
3. travel — married
4. rent — a car
5. have — around the world

2 Categorize the collocations from Activity 1 in the chart below.

Personal Development	Financial Security
travel around the world	

3 Complete the sentences with the collocations below.

~~be more patient~~   save resources   take a gap year   get a job
start my own business   go to vocational school

0. I often get frustrated when things don't go my way. I want to _____be more patient_____.
1. I've always been very motivated to succeed and I love business. I want to _____.
2. I know I want to go to college, but I'm not sure I'm ready yet. I may _____.
3. I love working with my hands, taking things apart and putting them back together. I might _____ to become an electrician or plumber.
4. I'm going to go to college before I _____ because I know I'll have more career opportunities with a degree.
5. I'm really worried about the environment, so I'm going to _____ like electricity and water.

4 Complete the collocation with the correct form of the verb and match each question to its answer.

0. Are you going to _____rent_____ an apartment next year? d
1. What are you _____ for? ___
2. Why do you want to _____ a healthier lifestyle? ___
3. Do you think you will _____ around the world? ___
4. Do you think _____ resources, like electricity, is important? ___
5. Will you _____ your own business some day? ___

a. I don't want to get diabetes when I get older.
b. I hope so! I want to learn about other cultures.
c. Of course! We all have to contribute to reducing climate change!
d. No, I'd rather buy a house.
e. I don't know. I might. Or I may work for a company.
f. I'll probably buy a car.

Grammar – Reported Speech

1 **Write sentences in the future continuous.**

0. What / you / do / tomorrow at 5 p.m. / ?   exercise / gym
   What will you be doing tomorrow at 5pm?   _I'll be exercising at the gym._

1. What / your sister / study / at college / next year / ?   study / law

2. What / classes / you / take / next semester / ?   take / social science and economics

3. Where / you / live / in a couple of years / ?   live / in the US

4. Who / wait / for you at the airport / ?   George / wait / for me

2 **Complete the sentences with the correct form of future continuous.**

0. By this time next year, _____I won't be attending_____ (attend ✗) high school any more.
1. When your plane gets in we _____ (wait ✓) for you.
2. Bethany _____ (come ✗) to the party because she has to work.
3. My cousins _____ (take ✓) a gap year after they graduate.
4. In five years I _____ (work ✓) in a successful company.
5. At 10 p.m., he _____ (study ✗); he'll be sleeping.

8 Unit

3 Look at the time line and write activities Sandra will be doing in the future.

She'll be walking in the park. _____ _____ _____

~~walk~~	go to college	working	live
next Tuesday	next year	in five years	in 10 years

4 Write about what you will be doing in the future.

My Future Plans
Next Tuesday, _____
Next year, _____
In five years, _____
In 10 years, _____

Review

1 Complete each sentence describing what Brad will be doing after he graduates from college.

0. One year after Brad graduates from college, _he will be traveling around the world_ .

1. Two years after Brad graduates from college, _____ _____ .

2. Three years after Brad graduates from college, _____ _____ .

3. Four years after Brad graduates from college, _____ _____ .

4. Five years after Brad graduates from college, _____ _____ .

5. Six years after Brad graduates from college, _____ _____ .

Reading

1 Answer the following questions T (True) or F (False) about your savings habits.

1. I have a part-time job or other way to make money.   T   F
2. I regularly save money.   T   F
3. I have a savings account at a bank.   T   F

The Power of Exponential Growth

Perhaps you have heard of the concept of exponential growth in your math class. Here's one important concept that applies to real life! It's very powerful and very important to consider when you save money.

What is exponential growth? The dictionary says it's development at an increasingly rapid rate in proportion to the growing total number or size. Basically, it means the bigger something is, the faster it grows.

Let's look at how it applies to savings. You go to the bank and open a **mutual fund** account. It may increase 10% a year. That means it could give you back 10% of what you put in each year. Say you save $100 in the first year. After one year, your **balance** is $110 and you didn't even add anything to it! One more year later you could earn $11 in interest since 10% of $111 is $11, so now your total is $121. This is money that you make only off the $100 that you started with.

Now imagine that you add to it every year. Let's say you have $100 to add each year and you deposit every year for 10 years. At the end of 10 years you have a balance of $1,593.00. That's $1,000 of money you put in and $593.00 in interest payments.

Of course once you graduate and start a full-time job, you can save even more. You just have to be patient, keep saving and watch your money grow!

Need an idea for how to make money now? Consider the following suggestions.
- Help out at the family business or at home. Ask your parents for an **allowance**.
- Get a part-time job at a fast food restaurant or a store at the mall.
- Tutor your classmates or younger kids for money.
- Babysit.
- Sell your old clothes or other items you no longer need.

Remember, the key is to save as much as you can as early as you can! Most banks will let you open a savings account that offers interest while you are still a teenager. Happy saving!

2 Answer the following questions in your notebook. Then share your answers with a parter.

1. What is exponential growth in your own words?
2. If you deposited $1,000 and got 10% interest annually, how much total money would you have after one year? After two years?
3. What kind of bank account can you open while you are still a teen?

Writing

3 Create a savings action plan in your notebook.

Include information about:
- Ways you can make money.
- Details about how much you will save and how often.
- Where you will save the money.
- What you will be doing to continue saving.

Glossary

mutual fund: an account that invests your money in multiple stocks and bonds

balance: the amount of money in your account.

allowance: an amount of money that is given to someone regularly or for a specific purpose

Just for Fun Answer Key

Unit 1
1 *Down:* 1. unreasonable 2. inconsiderate 5. dishonest;
Across: 3. irresponsible 4. unfriendly 6. impatient
2 Answers will vary.
3 Answers will vary.

Unit 2
1 hammer, saw, hot glue gun, screwdriver, nails, glue stick
2 drill, solder, screws, plywood, soldering iron
3 To invent, you need a good imagination and a pile of junk.

Unit 3
1 Alex developed a computer game at school.
I don't think Laura Dekker has written a book about her solo circumnavigation.
Alice hasn't gotten a part-time job yet, but she'll keep looking.
Dennis and Jill have been attending acting classes for a year.
My cousin Will has started a band with friends.
My sister has been traveling alone around Asia for two months now.
Some of my classmates have created a vlog about DIY tips for girls.
My father has been building a drone since last summer.
My mom wants to learn a foreign language.

Unit 4
1 1. car pool 2. reusable shopping bag 3. electric bike 4. vinegar, baking soda 5. indoor garden 6. reusable batteries 7. food leftovers
2 1. will find 2. fall 3. would, think 4. Would, stand up 5. lose 6. will be 7. walk 8. Would, dance, Would 9. look 10. saw, Would 11. save

Unit 5
1 *Supernatural Creatures:* alien, werewolf, zombie, ghost
ESP: telepathy, clairvoyance, telekinesis
2 1. T 2. F 3. F 4. T 5. T 6. T
3 Answers will vary.
4 Answers will vary.

Unit 6
1 1. disaster 2. crisis 3. pandemic 4. revolution 5. breakthrough 6. war
Mystery Word: discovery
2 1. Pompeii was a Roman city.
4. The American Revolution took place between 1765 and 1783.
3 That's one small step for man, one giant leap for mankind.

Unit 7
1 1. visa 2. buy plane tickets 3. language school 4. course 5. new friends
Mystery sentence: The world is a book and those who do not travel read only a page.
2 Answers will vary.
3 Answers will vary.

Unit 8
1 1. lifestyle 2. patient 3. vocational 4. business 5. apartment 6. world 7. money 8. married
2 1. l 2. i 3. v 4. i 5. n 6. g 7. c 8. h 9. i 10. n 11. a
Complete sentence: Nick will be living in China by this time next year.

Grammar Reference

Tag Questions

We use tag questions to make comments about a situation or check if a piece of information is correct:

- *Bea Parker is friendly, **isn't she**?* (The speaker is making a comment about Bea Parker's personality.)
- *She didn't go for an interview at a school, **did she**?* (The speaker is checking if Bea went for an interview at a school.)

To form the tag question, we always use an auxiliary or modal verb, or a form of *be*. The use depends on the verb form in the statement.

- *You **are** very patient, **aren't** you?*
- *Bea **has** a few hours free each month, **doesn't** she?*
- *You **didn't send** a message to Steven Porter, **did** you?*
- *The volunteer **won't clean** the kennels, **will** he?*
- *Steven **has worked** for Happy Paws, **hasn't** he?*
- *People **can** visit Happy Paws, **can't** they?*

Look at the tag question for *I am*.

- *I'm a good candidate for the position, **aren't I**?*

The tag question always follows a statement. If the verb in the statement is in the affirmative form, the tag is negative; if the verb in the statement is in the negative form, the tag is affirmative.

Statement	Tag Question
Responsible people **make** good volunteers,	don't they?
Honest people **don't tell** lies,	do they?

We always use a pronoun in the tag question. If the subject of the statement is *this* or *that*, we use *it* in the tag question.

- ***Steven Porter** didn't interview many candidates, did **he**?*
- ***Bea Parker** was one of the candidates, wasn't **she**?*
- ***This** is a very serious and efficient NGO, isn't **it**?*

The intonation of your voice varies in tag questions. If you are making comments or checking information, the intonation of your voice falls at the tag question.

- *The volunteer job at Happy Paws is interesting, **isn't it?*** (The speaker is making a comment.)
- *Ben has enjoyed teaching IT to older adults, **hasn't he?*** (The speaker doesn't have the information.)

160

Passive Voice

We use the passive voice when:

- We want to focus on the event (what is happening or the action), and not on the agent (who or what did the action).
- *Drones **are being used** by military forces.* (The use of drones is more important than who is using them.)
- We don't know who the agent is, or there isn't an agent.
- *Nikola Tesla's achievements **were forgotten**.* (We don't know who forgot his achievements.)
- It is clear from the context who the agent is.
- *Virgin Galactic is planning suborbital flights for tourists. Over 700 tickets **have been sold**.* (It is clear that Virgin Galactic has sold the tickets.)

We form the passive voice with a form of *be* + past participle of main verb:

- *Virgin Galactic **was founded** in 2004.*
- *Quadcopters **can be made** at home.*

- *Drones **will be used** to deliver packages in the near future.*
- *Sir Richard Branson **has been awarded** several prizes.*

When the agent is included in statements in the passive voice, we use *by* to introduce it.

- *Virgin Galactic was founded in 2004 **by Sir Richard Branson**.*
- *Quadcopters can be made at home **by hobbyists**.*
- *Drones will be used **by Amazon** to deliver packages in the near future.*
- *Sir Richard Branson has been awarded several prizes **by different institutions**.*

Unit 3

Present Perfect vs. Present Perfect Continuous

We often use the present perfect for actions that have already finished.

- **I've visited** Italy. (I visited the country and now I am back home.)
- Tyler Smith **has gone** for a job interview. (The interview is over.)
- Julia Stevenson **has** already **packed**. (Her suitcases are ready.)

We use the present perfect continuous for actions that started in the past and are still in progress in the present.

- Julia **has been traveling** around Italy. (She started her trip some time ago, and is still traveling.)
- Tyler **has been looking** for a job. (He started looking for a job some time ago, and he doesn't have a job yet.)

We form the present perfect with *have / has* + past participle form of main verb.

- Julia **has taken** lots of pictures of Venice.

The present perfect continuous is formed with *have/has* + *been* + *-ing* form of main verb.

- Tyler and Alice **have been practicing** job interview questions.

In the present perfect continuous, we use **since** to say **when** the action in progress started, and **for** to say **how long** it has been happening.

- Tyler has been looking for a job **since February**.

since + moment in time

- Julia has been traveling around Italy **for two weeks**.

for + period of time

With verbs that suggest continuity (e.g., *like, live, sleep, study, work*), we can use the present perfect with *since* and *for*, even if the action is in progress.

- Alice **has liked** Tyler **for a long time**, but he doesn't know that.
- Shh! Julia **has slept** on the train **since the beginning of the trip**!

First Conditional

We use the first conditional to say **what will happen in the future if certain conditions are met**.

- *If you ride your bike to school, you will reduce CO2 emissions.* (In order to reduce CO2 emissions, you need to ride your bike to school.)
- *People will have fewer health problems if pollution levels are reduced.* (In order to improve people's health, pollution levels needed to be reduced.)

In first conditional sentences, the *if* **clause states the condition**, while the **future clause presents the result**. We use the **simple present** in the *if* clause and **will** or **going to + verb** in the result clause.

Condition	Result
If Eric **gets** an electric bike for Christmas,	he **won't take** a bus to school anymore.
If you **go** to school by yourself,	your parents **are going to be** happy.

We can also use a modal verb in the result clause.

- *If we organize a car pool to school, we **might have** five or six people in the car.*
- *If Alice wants to start a community garden, she **needs to learn** about gardening.*

We can start first conditional sentences with the result clause. When beginning the conditional sentence with the *if* clause, use a comma to separate it from the result clause.

- *If you go to school by bike, you will save gas and money.*
- *You will save gas and money if you go to school by bike.*

Second Conditional

We use the second conditional to talk about **unreal or imaginary conditions and their results in the present**.

- *If plastic bags were banned all over the world, we would have much less trash in the oceans.* (Plastic bag aren't banned all over the world and we have a lot of trash in the oceans.)
- *Students would recycle their trash at our school if we had recycling bins.* (We don't have recycling bins at our school, so students don't recycle their trash.)

In second conditional sentences, the *if* **clause states the unreal condition**, while the **other clause presents the result**. We use the **simple past** in the *if* clause and **would + verb** in the result clause.

Condition	Result
If I **cleaned** my house,	I **would use** vinegar and baking soda.
If our family **didn't grow** vegetables,	we **would buy** them at a grocery store.

Note: Although we use the simple past in the *if* clause, the meaning of second conditional sentences is not in the past. In *if* clauses, we use *were* for all subjects.

- *If I **were** you, I'd stop using plastic bags.*
- *I would buy an electric car if it **were** cheaper.*

We can also use a modal verb in the result clause.

- *If Jack found a part-time job, he **could save** some money to buy an electric car.*

We can start second conditional sentences with the result clause. When beginning the conditional sentence with the *if* clause, use a comma to separate it from the result clause.

- *If we stopped using plastic bags, tons of resources would be saved.*
- *Tons of resources would be saved if we stopped using plastic bags.*

Unit 5

Modals of Speculation – Past: *must have*, *might have* and *could have*

We use *must have*, *might have* and *could have* to make informed guesses about situations in the past. The choice of the modal depends on how certain we are about these guesses.

must have might have could have	Certain ↕ Uncertain	could not have must not have might not have

We use **must have** when **we are almost sure** something happened.
- Emily **must have driven** to school before she disappeared. Her car is in the parking lot.

When **we are slightly less sure** something happened, we use **might have**.
- Emily **might have taken** her cell phone with her, or she **might have left** it in the car.

We use **could have** when **we are even less sure** something happened.
- Although we talked to most of her friends, Emily **could have gone** to someone's house.

We use **could not have** when **we are almost sure** something didn't happen.
- Emily **couldn't have gone** far. She had very little money on her.

When **we are slightly less sure** something didn't happen, we use **must not have**.
- Emily **must not have been** kidnapped.

We use **might not have** when **we are even less sure** something didn't happen.
- Emily **might not have run** away from home.

To speculate about the past, we use a modal verb + (*not*) + *have* + past participle or main verb.
- Different civilizations **might have built** Stonehenge over the centuries.
- Artifacts show that rich or religious people **must have been buried** at Stonehenge.
- Stonehenge **couldn't have been built** by aliens, as some people claim.

Unit 6

Third Conditional

We use the **third conditional** to discuss **unreal or imaginary conditions in the past and their unreal results in the past**.

- If the American army hadn't dropped the atomic bombs on Japan, thousands of Japanese people wouldn't have died. (The American army dropped the atomic bombs on Japan and thousands of people died.)
- Katie wouldn't have traveled to France if her mom hadn't paid for the trip. (Katie's mom paid for the trip and she traveled to France.)

In third conditional sentences, the *if* **clause states the unreal condition in the past**, while the **other clause presents the unreal result**. We use the **past perfect** in the *if* clause and **would** + **have** + **past participle** in the result clause.

Condition	Result
If men **hadn't gone** to the moon,	we **wouldn't have gotten** information about lunar soil.
If I **had moved** to another country,	I **wouldn't have met** my best friend.

We can also use a modal verb in the result clause.

- If something had gone wrong on Apolo 11, the astronauts **could have died**.

We can start third conditional sentences with the result clause. When beginning the conditional sentence with the *if* clause, use a comma to separate it from the result clause.

- If Apple had gone bankrupt in the 1990s, the iPhone wouldn't have been invented.
- The iPhone wouldn't have been invented if Apple had gone bankrupt in the 1990s.

Mixed Conditionals

It is possible to mix tenses in conditional structures to talk about conditions and results in different moments in time.

- If Steve Jobs hadn't died, would Apple be a different company today? (condition in the past; result in the present)
- If you were a nicer person, you wouldn't have been so rude to Melissa. (condition in the present; result in the past)

Condition	Result
If computers **hadn't been invented**, had + past participle	life **would be** very different nowadays. would + verb
If I **had** more time to study, simple past	I **wouldn't have failed** the history test. would + have + past participle

Unit 7

Reported Speech

We use reported speech to **share what another speaker said, without using the exact words**.

- Katie: *"I'll study French in France in the summer."*
  Katie said she would study French in France in the summer.

- Jake: *"I'm in love with you, Katie."*
  Jake told Katie he's in love with her.

To introduce the reported statement, we use verbs such as *say*, *tell*, *ask* and *invite* in the simple past. We can use *that* after *say* and *tell*.

Note: we use *say* when the interlocutor is not mentioned.

- *Emily told Jake that he was silly sometimes.*
- *Emily said that he was silly sometimes.*
- *Emily said he was silly sometimes.*

In reported speech, the verb tense usually "goes one tense back" in the past. Modal verbs change as well.

Direct speech	Reported speech
Simple present	Simple past
Present continuous	Past continuous
Simple past	Past perfect
Present perfect	Past perfect
Will	Would
Can	Could
May	Might
Must	Had to

We don't change verb tenses in reported speech when:

- the fact being reported is a general truth.
  Our teacher said water boils at 100°C.

- reporting something a person has just said.
  Louise said the bus is coming.

- reporting something that is still true.
  Jake told Emily he doesn't want her to go to France.

When reporting imperative statements, use (*not*) + *to* infinitive.

- Emily: *"Talk to Katie about how you feel, Jake!"*
  *Emily told Jake **to talk** to Katie about how he feels.*

- Jake: *"Don't go to France, Katie!"*
  *Jake asked Katie **not to go** to France.*

In reported speech, other words also change in the sentence:

- Pronouns and possessive adjectives.
  Katie: *"I'd like my passport, please."*
  *Katie said **she**'d like **her** passport.*

- Time phrases.
  Katie: *"Jake, I'm going to travel next week."*
  *Katie told Jake she's going to travel **the following week**.*

Unit 8

Future Continuous

We use the future continuous to talk about actions in progress at a certain time in the future.

- *Cameron **will be living** in Africa in ten years' time.*
- *Mackenzie **will be running** her own restaurant in ten years' time.*

The future continuous is formed with *will + be + -ing* form of main verb. To make a sentence negative, add *not* to *will*.

- *I **will be studying** at a good university at this time next year.*
- *James **will not be working** during the weekend.*

To form Yes / No questions, we put *will* before the subject. To ask for information, we use *wh-* words.

- ***Will** you **be traveling** during your gap year?*
- *What **will** Ann **be doing** in five years' time?*

We use the future continuous with time expressions such as *while, when, this time (tomorrow), in (ten) years' time, at this time (next year),* and others.

Verb List

Base Form	Past	Past Participle	Base Form	Past	Past Participle
abduct	abducted	abducted	laugh	laughed	laughed
answer	answered	answered	learn	learned	learned
apply	applied	applied	like	liked	liked
arrest	arrested	arrested	live	lived	lived
ask	asked	asked	make	made	made
attend	attended	attended	manufacture	manufactured	manufactured
bake	baked	baked	meet	met	met
be	was / were	been	melt	melted	melted
become	became	become	miss	missed	missed
behave	behaved	behaved	play	played	played
break	broke	broke	produce	produced	produced
bring	brought	brought	record	recorded	recorded
build	built	built	rent	rented	rented
buy	bought	bought	ride	rode	ridden
care	cared	cared	rise	rose	risen
carry	carried	carried	run	ran	run
choose	chose	chosen	save	saved	saved
clean	cleaned	cleaned	say	said	said
crash	crashed	crashed	see	saw	seen
depict	depicted	depicted	sell	sold	sold
develop	developed	developed	send	sent	sent
die	died	died	show	showed	shown
do	did	done	sneak	sneaked	sneaked
draw	drew	drawn	spend	spent	spent
drop	dropped	dropped	study	studied	studied
eat	ate	eaten	take	took	taken
enjoy	enjoyed	enjoyed	tell	told	told
enroll	enrolled	enrolled	think	thought	thought
fall	fell	fallen	throw	threw	thrown
feed	fed	fed	tour	toured	toured
fight	fought	fought	travel	traveled	traveled
find	found	found	try	tried	tried
forget	forgot	forgotten	wake	woke	waken
found	founded	founded	win	won	won
get	got	gotten	work	worked	worked
give	gave	given	write	wrote	written
go	went	gone			
grow	grew	grown			
happen	happened	happened			
have	had	had			
help	helped	helped			
hire	hired	hired			
hit	hit	hit			
join	joined	joined			
keep	kept	kept			
know	knew	known			

168